THE LITTLE GIANT BOOK® OF
ANIMAL FACTS

by Glen Vecchione

Sterling Publishing Co., Inc.
New York

To Gina Alexander and her staff
at the Marina Pacifica Barnes & Noble:
Dedicated booklovers, all.

Library of Congress Cataloging-in-Publication Data

10 9 8 7 6 5 4 3 2 1

Vecchione, Glen.
Little giant book of animal facts / Glen Vecchione ; illustrated by
Joel & Sharon Harris.
     v. cm.
   Includes index.
   Contents: Curious canines—Wings and feathers—Creatures of the
deep—Jungle giants—Brains and beauty—Insect invasion—Woodsy
wild things—Reptilian relations—Dinosaurs and other extinct animals.
   ISBN 1-4027-0785-1
   1. Animals—Miscellanea—Juvenile literature. [1. Animals—Miscellanea.]
I. Harris, Joel, 1969- ill. II. Harris, Sharon, 1971- ill. III. Title.
QL49 .V366 2004
590—dc22

                                                    2003024866

Published by Sterling Publishing Co., Inc.
387 Park Avenue South, New York, NY 10016
© 2004 by Glen Vecchione
Distributed in Canada by Sterling Publishing
ᶜ/₀ Canadian Manda Group, One Atlantic Avenue, Suite 105
Toronto, Ontario, Canada M6K 3E7
Distributed in Great Britain and Europe by Chris Lloyd at Orca Book Services,
Stanley House, Fleets Lane, Poole BH15 3AJ, England
Distributed in Australia by Capricorn Link (Australia) Pty. Ltd.,
P.O. Box 704, Windsor, NSW 2756, Australia

Printed in China
All rights reserved

Sterling ISBN 1-4027-0785-1

CONTENTS

Introduction

In this book you'll find more than 1,000 interesting facts about animals—familiar, not-so-familiar, unusual, and just plain bizarre. Whether you're curious about cats, millipedes, parakeets, porpoises, moles, or even the giant Mola mola fish—*The Little Giant® Book of Animal Facts* is sure to make you say "Wow!"

So why do people love facts? Probably because facts are like little stories. They can tell us something new about a subject we thought we already knew all about. Or they can tell us something new, period. Having lots of unusual facts in your head makes you seem smart and interesting. And using a well-chosen fact to start a conversation is a great way to make a new friend or amuse an old one. So try out some of these:

- The forked tongue of a snake allows it to smell "in stereo."
- The lungs of a horse are three times larger than the lungs of a lion.
- Belching cows contribute to the "greenhouse effect" by adding methane to the atmosphere.

We think your friends will be begging for more. You can be sure that *The Little Giant® Book of Animal Facts* will keep you well-supplied for years to come with fascinating facts about the creatures that surround us.

FELINE FACTS

Think you know all about that purring critter curled up at your feet? Think again. We'll bet you hadn't a clue that your tabby was blessed by a prophet, sported a third eyelid, and had "furnishings" in its ear. And then there's the tabby's wilder relatives . . . let's just say that you wouldn't want some of *them* curled up at your feet! Read on and learn more.

Cats outnumber dogs as the preferred pet in America. There are about 66 million cats to 58 million dogs, with parakeets a distant third at 14 million.

Studies conducted at the University of Michigan showed that cats have better short-term memory than dogs. Tests were given that demonstrated that while a dog's memory of something lasts no more than 20 minutes, a cat's can last as long as 16 hours—even longer than the memories of monkeys and orangutans.

During an archeological excavation at Beni Hassan in Egypt in 1888, about 300,000 mummified cats were found in a tomb. The cat mummies were sold for $18.43 per ton and shipped to England to be ground up and used for fertilizer.

For the ancient Egyptians, the loss of a cat was a significant event, and all the members of the family would shave their eyebrows in mourning.

Healthy cats spend 15 percent of their lives in deep sleep. They spend as much as 50 percent of their lives in light sleep.

Cats were blamed for spreading the Black Death across England, and thousands were slaughtered. But people who kept their cats were less likely to catch the plague because their pets kept their houses free of rats—the real disease-carriers.

The average life span of a domestic cat is 12 years.

Cats lack the taste buds that detect sweets, but seem to enjoy them anyhow. The explanation? They probably detect the salty and sour underflavors.

JUST THE RIGHT TOUCH

Only a mother cat can safely pick up a kitten by the loose skin at the back of its neck. The mother's jaws grab just enough skin with just enough pressure to avoid hurting the kitten.

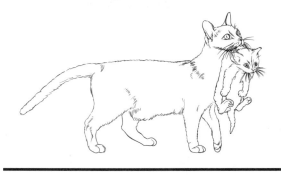

Cats will not walk on aluminum foil.

Cats' brains weigh about one percent of their total weight. Human brains weigh two percent of our total weight.

Catnip, a leafy herb in the mint family, affects all cats from the domestic variety to lions. A chemical in catnip, *nepetalactone*, stimulates pleasure-producing nerves in the cat's brain and causes the cat to roll, rub, drool, and wallow in the herb. After about 15 minutes, the effect wears off.

Some cats are completely immune to catnip's effects. Kittens are not affected by catnip until they are about three months old.

In humans, catnip tea induces sleep.

A cat's tongue resembles "Velcro" in that it consists of tiny elevated backward hooks, or papillae, that help tear up food.

A cat's purr has the same frequency as an idling diesel engine—about 26 cycles per second.

Cats frequently develop freckles. These can appear anywhere on the cat's skin, including inside their ears and mouth.

SMALL LUNGS, BIG APPETITE

Plant-eating horses have lungs three times the size of those in large, meat-eating cats like lions and tigers. This is because horses need larger lungs for long periods of aerobic activity, like running. Lions and tigers rely more on short bursts of anaerobic energy for jumping and pouncing—which use less oxygen.

Even the most placid household cat is not truly domesticated. Cats never truly lose their predatory instincts, even when born and raised in a human household. A cat that escapes into the wild has a much greater chance of survival than a domesticated dog.

"Mascara lines" are the dark lines that run together above a cat's eyes.

In some cultures, the black cat represents good fortune.

Although they prefer to vocalize, cats can also signal emotions with their tails. A cat twitches its tail to warn predators and tucks it close to its body when feeling threatened.

Cats have special cushions on their front paws that keep them from losing their balance. Called "carpal pads," they keep the cat from sliding on a slippery surface when jumping.

Catgut, once used in stringed instruments and tennis rackets, actually came from sheep, hogs, and horses.

During the reign of Kublai Khan, the Chinese used lions on hunting expeditions. They trained them to chase and drag down large animals, like bears and bulls, and stay with the kill until the hunting party arrived.

SAD SIGHT

The expression "raining cats and dogs" comes from 17th century England. During heavy downpours, stray animals often drowned, and their bodies would float in the rain torrents that flowed through the streets. This gave the appearance that it had literally rained "cats and dogs."

A cat's eyes will reveal its mood. A scared or excited cat will have large rounded pupils, and an angry cat will have narrow, slit-shaped pupils. The size of the pupils is related as much to a cat's mood as to the degree of light.

The term ailurophile refers to a cat-lover; an ailurophobe is one who fears cats. Julius Caesar, Henry II, Charles XI, Napoleon, Adolph Hitler, and Benito Mussolini were all ailurophobic.

Cats have over 100 vocal sounds. Dogs have about 30.

An adult domestic cat has 30 teeth.

A cat has 230 bones in its body, most of which are concentrated in its tail. A human being has 206 bones, most of which are in the spine.

SPACE SENSORS

Cats have four rows of whiskers (vibrissae). Combined in length, they equal the widest part of the cat's body. Cats and dogs use whiskers to test the width of a space before they attempt to crawl through it.

When a cat licks its paw after a fight with another animal, the animal is soothing itself by doing something natural and instinctive. After being handled, cats will also lick themselves to get rid of the "human" smell.

Experiments have shown that cats have some sensitivity to colors—mostly in the blue and yellow spectrum. This type of color vision is called "bichromatic" and is similar to the color vision of dogs. Humans, on the other hand, have trichromatic vision, allowing us to see all the visible colors and shades of the spectrum.

Cats have a third, hidden eyelid called a haw. The haw is exposed when the cat is nodding off or not feeling well.

A cat may have difficulty finding a food scrap on the floor because cats can't see directly under their noses.

A cat can arch its back because its spine contains nearly 60 vertebrae that fit loosely together. Humans have only 34 vertebrae. The arching makes the animal look larger and more threatening.

A cat's turning around and around before lying down is an instinct left over from the days when they slept in tall grass. The turning action pushed the grass down into a nest.

Aging cats can get "liver spots"—black patches on the skin that appear around the lips, eyes, and nose.

During medieval times in England, it was the custom to bury a cat alive in the wall of a newly constructed building for good luck. The practice was believed to ensure the structure's strength.

Often, cats are born with extra toes. Called polydactyl cats, they're often the result of too much inbreeding. Most "normal" cats have five toes on each front paw and four toes on each back paw.

PAPA HEMINGWAY'S CATS

The former Key West house of author Ernest Hemingway has about 60 resident cats—all the descendents of Boise and Princessa, the original Persians. Most of these offspring are polydactyl.

Cats have true fur, which means that they have both an undercoat and an outercoat.

Felix the Cat was the first cartoon character to ever have been made into a balloon for the Macy's Thanksgiving Day parade in 1927.

The darker patches of fur on a Siamese cat are due to lower body temperatures in those areas. These cats are born pure white because of the heat in the uterus, but their fur begins to darken only a few days after birth.

A cat's tail keeps it balanced and upright. The tail plays an important role in the "righting reflex" that helps a cat land on its feet when falling.

The domestic cat is the only species that can hold its tail vertically while walking. The wild cat holds its tail horizontally or tucked between its legs.

The African wild cat, still found in West Africa, is the ancestor of all domestic cats.

Domestic cats are skillful hunters, with one pounce in three resulting in a successful catch.

For a hungry cat, an average portion of canned or dry cat meal is roughly equivalent to five mice.

Every year, Americans spend about $1.5 billion on pet food—four times the amount spent on baby food.

Cats crave fats in their food because they cannot produce fats on their own. Calories stored in fat are one of the chief sources of a cat's energy and alertness.

The best litterbox arrangement for a multicat household is one box per cat, plus an extra box.

Cats bury their stools to cover their trail from predators.

Cats have a keen sense of smell and use another organ in addition to their noses. Called the Jacobson organ, it's located on the upper surface of the cat's mouth.

Cats have AB blood groups, just like people.

Cat allergies in humans are really a sensitivity to cat saliva or cat dander. If the cat is groomed regularly, the allergy is lessened.

Cat scratch disease, a painful inflammation of the skin, is caused by bacteria that live on the claws of the cat. But the disease can be transmitted by any clawed animal.

Like people, cats can be lacto-intolerant. This means that ingesting cows' milk gives them diarrhea.

A cat will develop either a left or right paw dominance.

A cat can jump up to eight times its height.

Cats lack a true collarbone; this helps them squeeze their upper bodies into small spaces.

Many white cats with blue eyes are deaf. White cats with only one blue eye are deaf in the ear closest to the blue eye.

The outer ear of a cat has 30 muscles that rotate it 180 degrees, so the cat can hear in all directions without turning its head. Human ears have only six muscles.

The long hairs that grow inside a cat's ears are called "furnishings." They help keep debris out of the cat's sensitive ear canals.

Newborn kittens are born with their ear canals sealed shut. The canals begin to open after about nine days.

With a topcoat five inches (12.7cm) long, the Persian cat has the longest, thickest fur of any domestic cat.

SHARP STRUTTIN'

Unlike any other domestic four-legged animals, cats walk directly on their claws and not on their paws. This kind of walking is called "digitigrade." When a cat scratches furniture, it's really tearing off the worn edges of its claws to sharpen them.

When walking or running, cats step with both left legs, and then with both right legs. The only other animals that do this are the giraffe and the camel.

According to a Christian folk story, a tabby cat purred the baby Jesus to sleep, and the Madonna was so pleased that she kissed the tabby on its forehead. Thereafter, all tabbies would have an "M" on their foreheads to show the Madonna's kiss.

Lions can eat everything from tortoises to giraffes, but develop an appetite for the specific type of prey they ate when they were growing up.

A group of lions is called a pride. Usually a lion pride consists of related females and two to three males. The number of animals varies anywhere from seven to twenty, but can get as large as forty.

Lions belonging to the same pride perform a greeting ritual upon meeting: they rub their heads and sides together, with tails looped high, while making friendly moaning sounds.

The territory of the pride is fixed, and its size depends on the availability of prey. In larger territories, which can be as much as 200 square miles, prides are often split into smaller social groups.

A lion chasing its prey can run the length of a football field in six seconds. Its eyes have a horizontal streak of nerve cells, which improves its vision following prey across a plain. Lions have taken down animals as large as buffaloes and giraffes.

Young male lions are banished from the pride at the age of about two years and then join a group of "bachelors." Each lion of this new group eventually tries to take over a pride by ousting an aging male.

Lions prefer a habitat of grasslands, savannas, woodlands, and dense brush. They seem to enjoy a geography of open space with occasional dense bushy areas for hiding and stalking.

The roar of an adult lion can be heard up to three miles (4.8km) away. It reunites scattered members of the pride, while warning intruders.

A full-grown lioness can weigh up to 270 pounds (122kg); a full-grown male weighs about 580 pounds (263kg).

None of a lion's teeth are good for chewing. It swallows its food in chunks.

A lion's life span ranges from 15 to 20 years.

A lioness will produce a litter that averages three or four cubs.

The adolescent male lion begins to grow his mane at about 18 months and it continues to grow until he reaches about five years of age. The mane darkens as he gets older.

A male lion's favorite activity is sleeping. He can spend up to 20 hours a day doing it.

The lioness is the "breadwinner" of the pride, bringing home the kill to her mate and cubs. The male lion is the first to eat, followed by the lioness. Whatever is left goes to the cubs.

A lion can eat up to 65 pounds (30kg) of meat per meal. They usually eat every two to three days, but can go without food for weeks.

A male lion will only hunt if he's without a mate.

Lions will sometimes try to steal prey from other predators like the cheetah, leopard, or hyena. A fierce battle may result, but the lion usually wins.

When food is scarce, lion cubs will sometimes starve as a result of being last in the pecking order.

Lions usually trap their prey by hiding in groups. A solitary lion will startle the prey from the opposite direction and chase it towards the waiting hunters.

An ambush hunt is successful about 30 percent of the time. A lone hunt results in a kill only 15 percent of the time.

In the past, lions could be found almost anywhere in Africa. Today they survive mostly in protected areas like Kenya's Amboseli Park.

A full-grown male lion can grow up to 10 feet (3m) in body length and is surpassed in size only by the largest species of tiger.

The male Siberian tiger is by far the largest and most powerful member of the cat family. It has a total body length in excess of 10 feet (3m) and weighs up to 661 pounds (300kg).

With the exception of the lion, the members of the cat family (*Felidae*) are solitary creatures.

Species of tiger (*Panthera tigris*) range from the small Bali tiger to the Siberian tiger, the largest cat in the world. All tigers are endangered and some species are extinct.

Tigers have striped skin, not just striped fur.

No two tigers have the same pattern of stripes, just as no two humans have the same fingerprints.

Of all tiger species, the Sumatran tiger has the most stripes and the Siberian tiger the fewest stripes.

Although a tiger's stripes seem spectacular to human eyes, the stripes help the animal hide because they blend in with tall plants and trees.

Tigers and housecats share similar teeth, claws, skull shape, and hunting methods.

"Pub marks" refer to a tiger's paw prints.

In general, the tiger is a forest dweller, but it can also be found in grasslands and swamps. It is never more than a few hours from a source of water.

All tigers are excellent swimmers and love bathing in pools and lakes in the hotter regions.

Tigers are nocturnal hunters, although in protected areas away from human activity the animal is often active during the day.

Tigers prefer large prey such as wild boar, buffalo, and deer, but also hunt fish, monkeys, and other small mammals if their preferred food is unavailable.

Tigers and the other big cats can only purr when breathing out. Small cats like our pets can purr when breathing both ways.

The tiger is often regarded as a cautious hunter, stalking as close as it can to the rear of its prey before making its final charge.

A tiger kills smaller prey with a single bite to the throat or neck, which severs the spinal cord. With larger animals, it bites the throat, pinching it closed until the animal suffocates.

Like many cats, the tiger hoards its food, returning to feed on a carcass over several days.

Although mostly a solitary animal, a male tiger will often share his food with other members of the family group. His mate eats next; his cubs eat last.

Male tigers can have a single mate or polygamous arrangements. In all cases, a male tiger defends his mates against other intruding males.

A tiger litter usually consists of about three cubs, which are born about four months after mating.

Young male cubs will stay with their mothers for up to two years, during which time they learn the skills of hunting. Female cubs stay close to their mothers for life, even after they find a mate.

THE RARE WHITE TIGER

The last sighting of a rare white tiger in the wild was in Central India in 1951. The male animal was captured by the Maharaja of Rewa and named "Mohan." Most of the white tigers we see in captivity today are descended from Mohan.

The white tiger is not a true albino but simply has less dark pigment in its coat. This is known as the "chinchilla mutation."

HIGH-LEAPING CAT

Servals are primarily crepuscular (active at dawn and dusk) but they may also be active in the daytime. They can run swiftly for short distances and make remarkable vertical jumps of up to 10 feet (3m) to catch birds. They also make arching leaps spanning up to 13 feet (4m) and over 3 feet (1m) high when hunting prey on the ground. Servals have good vision and hearing.

The cheetah is the only feline in the world that can't retract its claws.

The cheetah is the fastest of all cats, with a top running speed of about 70 miles (113km) per hour. It can't sustain that speed for long, however, and so it stalks its prey to get as close as it can before breaking into a run.

Unlike most other cats, the cheetah hunts almost entirely in the daytime.

The cheetah successfully lands its prey about 40 percent of the time.

A cheetah's bark resembles the chirp of a bird or the yelp of a dog. The sound is so penetrating that it can be heard up to a mile (1.6km) away.

The leopard has the most widespread distribution of all the cats. It can be found in India, Africa, China, Siberia, and Korea.

Leopards live for 10 to 15 years in the wild, although in captivity they can live for up to 20 years.

An adult male leopard weighs about 176 pounds (80kg).

Leopards can live without water for long periods of time, getting their liquid from prey, such as gazelles, antelopes, monkeys, insects, snakes, sheep, and goats.

Leopards sometimes take their kill up into trees to protect it from hyenas and lions. They can lift a carcass up to three times their body weight and have been seen hauling young giraffes up into trees.

Almost half of all leopard cubs born do not reach adulthood. They are easy prey for lions and other large, carnivorous cats.

The same species of leopard can show a great variety in size, depending on how much prey is available throughout a region.

Leopard cubs are born blind and stay with their mothers until they are about 18 months old. The father does not participate in rearing the cubs.

Snow leopards, mountain cats of central Asia, are an endangered species.

The largest cat of the Americas, the jaguar, is called the "eater of souls" by the Yanomami Indians because they believe it consumes the spirits of the dead.

The jaguar is distinguished from the leopard by the irregular shapes within larger round markings, a larger and stockier head and body, and a shorter tail.

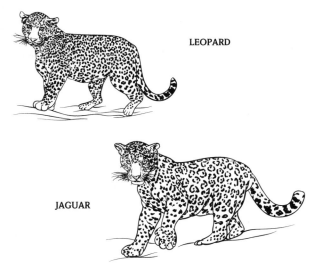

LEOPARD

JAGUAR

Jaguars range from the southwest and Mexico, to Central and South America. Highest population densities are found in the lowland rain forests of the Amazon Basin.

Jaguars are not nocturnal and tend to hunt between dawn and dusk. They kill their prey by piercing the skull with their sharp incisor teeth.

A jaguar in water will sometimes use the tip of its tail to lure fish close to the surface, where the jaguar can grab them.

The Olmecs, the earliest known Mexican civilization, believed in "were-jaguars," a man-jaguar transformation with characteristics of both. Were-jaguars were though to be the forerunners of Aztec and Mayan rain gods.

Jaguars are solitary and meet only to mate. They are the least understood of all the big cats.

Jaguars can live for 11 to 12 years in the wild and 20 years in captivity.

WHAT'S THAT CAT?

Mountain lion, puma, cougar, panther—this cat is known by more names than just about any other mammal! How did it get so many names? Mostly because it has such a wide range, and people from different countries have called it different things. Early Spanish explorers in North and South America called it *leon* (lion) and *gato monte* (cat of the mountain), from which we get the name mountain lion. Puma is the name the Incas gave this cat in their language. Cougar seems to have come from an old South American Indian word, *cuguacuarana*, which was shortened to *cuguar* and then spelled differently. And panther is a general term for cats that have solid-colored coats, so it was used for pumas as well as black jaguars. All of these names are considered correct, but scientists usually use the name puma.

A panther is actually a completely black leopard or jaguar. Panthers can be born in the same litter as the usual spotted leopards and jaguars. They are found more often in the dense forest areas of India and other parts of Asia, where the dark coat is a better camouflage.

How well do we know our best friend? For all their familiar appeal, dogs have a secret and mysterious side filled with instincts and urges inherited from their distant, and not so friendly, ancestors. Find out what that wagging tail really means!

Dogs are part of the family Canidae, which includes wolves, coyotes, and foxes. Zoologists believe they evolved about 60 million years ago.

Gray wolves (*Canis lupus*) are the ancestors of all domestic dogs. They entered villages in the Northern Hemisphere in search of food about 12,000 years ago.

The gray wolves have a keen sense of smell and hunt large prey such as moose, reindeer, elk, and bison.

The intelligence and sociability of gray wolves encouraged early humans to use them to guard, herd, and hunt. Particular traits of a wolf were encouraged by selective breeding, which began the diversity in breeds we see today.

Today, canids are found in the wild on all the continents except Antarctica and occupy a variety of habitats including grassland, temperate forest, rainforest, desert, mountain regions, and tundra.

The average life span of a dog is from 7 to 18 years, with larger dogs having shorter lives.

Salivation does not substitute for sweating in a dog. Dogs do sweat—through the pads of their feet.

Although the human nose has about 5 million olfactory cells, the sheepdog has 220 million, allowing it to smell 44 times better than a human.

A poll conducted by the American Animal Hospital Association showed that 33 percent of dog owners talk to their dogs on the phone or leave messages on an answering machine while away.

FANCY HUNTERS

France is not the country of origin of the famous French poodle. The poodle was originally raised as a hunting dog in Germany and England. Since its thick coat often got snared in the brush, hunters sheared the hindquarters and left cuffs around the ankles, in the "French style," to protect against rheumatism. Hunters would also distinguish the dogs of one hunting party from another by tying bright ribbons around the head of each member of the poodle pack.

The first paintings of domesticated dogs were found on an Egyptian drinking cup from the Badarian age (5,500–4,000 B.C.), but it's difficult to recognize the breeds. Paintings of dogs with collars were found on stone tablets dating from about 1,000 years later.

One of the oldest dog breeds in recorded history is the greyhound, dating back to the Predynastic Period of ancient Egypt (3,500–3,000 B.C).

Close contenders to the oldest breed of dog (greyhound) are the Saluki and Afghan, dating back about 5,000 years to ancient Sumeria. Archeologists recognized both breeds from temple carvings.

The dachshund was domesticated about 3,000 years ago in Egypt. But the Medieval Germans gave it its name, which means "hunter of badgers."

The dachshund is the smallest breed of dog used for hunting. Its short length and low body allows it to enter and maneuver through tunnels easily.

Selective inbreeding of dogs has created problems. For example, the dachshund's spine, now too long to comfortably support the weight of its body, can be a source of discomfort for the animal.

In the mid-1800s, dalmatians were trained to run alongside horses and carriages, protecting the passengers from other dogs who would chase the entourage. Because of this function, they became known as "carriage dogs."

Dalmatians were also used to keep other dogs away from racing fire engines, and became known as the mascot dogs of the fire service.

Recent experiments show that dogs can perform a certain degree of quantitative analysis. When a dog was fed 10 small treats repeatedly, and then only seven treats, the dog waited for the remaining three before turning away.

Most of the dog breeds we know today began in the 19th century. Breeders carefully selected mating pairs so that the litters would have particular traits thought desirable by dog owners.

The chihuahua is both the smallest and the longest-living breed of dog, with a life span of 12 to 20 years. The breed was named for the region of Mexico where they were first discovered, domesticated, and eaten!

Chihuahuas are clannish, preferring their own kind. As a rule, they do not like dogs of other breeds.

Short-snouted dogs were popular as pets in the 19th century, and breeders accentuated this trait. The result was several breeds of dogs, such as pugs and Pekinese, with extremely short snouts—so short, in fact, that their abbreviated windpipes can lead to breathing difficulties.

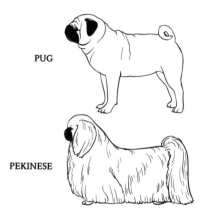

PUG

PEKINESE

Short-snouted dogs were popular among the childless European aristocracy because they were thought to resemble human babies.

The term "dog days" dates back to Roman times and refers to the midsummer period from July 3 to August 11. During this time it was believed that Sirius, the Dog Star, added its heat to the heat of the sun. The Romans called these weeks *dies caniculares* or "days of the dog."

Dogs detect moving images better than still ones.

Dogs can't focus clearly on objects closer than 20 inches (50cm), and at four inches (10cm), they can hardly see a thing. Your face is a total blur to your doggy when he's slathering you with kisses.

A dog has various ways of wagging its tail to indicate its mood. A high, brisk, circular wag means excitement, while a low side-to-side wag means "come no closer." A shivering wag with the tail tucked under the hind legs indicates fear or submission.

German shepherds are more prone to nearsightedness than other breeds; American cocker spaniels are more prone to glaucoma. Most dog vision problems are the result of too much inbreeding.

Dogs have only two kinds of color sensing cells, or cones, in their eyes. The cones sense hues of yellow and blue the best. Dogs can detect red and green but, like a person with red-green color blindness, can't distinguish between them.

Korea's *poshintang*—dog meat soup—is a popular summer dish, despite protests by animal rights groups. The soup is believed to improve male virility and women's complexions.

The bloodhound is the only animal whose evidence is admissible in an American court.

RED-EYED CANINES

The *tapetum lucidum* is a layer of cells under a dog's retina that helps it see in dim light. If a ray of light passes through the retina without getting absorbed by the rods and cones, it reflects off the tapetum and back to the retina for a second chance. (The *tapetum lucidum* also causes the eyes of dogs, cats, and many other night creatures to gleam orange in the dark.) But although the tapetum enhances low-light vision, it has a disadvantage, too. When light bounces back, its source is less precise, so dogs have only about 20:75 vision. This means that a sign a human could read at 75 feet could only be read at 20 feet (6m) by a dog—that is, if a dog could read!

Dogs have more rods, cells that detect light from dark, than people do. This means that they can see about six times better than people at dawn, dusk, and nighttime.

A chemical in chocolate, *theobromine*, stimulates the heart and nervous systems of dogs, especially pups. Just a few grams of milk chocolate or cooking chocolate (which contains more theobromine per gram) can cause convulsions and a heart attack.

There are 701 types of purebred dogs.

The United States has more than 100 million dogs and cats. Americans spend more than 5.4 billion dollars on their pets each year.

The term "three dog night" comes from the Australian Aborigines. It refers to a night so cold that an Aborigine would have to bed down with three wild dogs, or dingoes, to keep warm.

The first seeing-eye dog was given to a blind person on April 25, 1938.

Jerome Napoleon Bonaparte, the last member of the famous Bonaparte family, died in 1945. His death was due to injuries sustained from tripping over his dog's leash.

Dogs are mentioned 14 times in the Bible.

"Millie," Barbara Bush's English springer spaniel, was the most popular "First Dog" in U.S. presidential history. Mrs. Bush's book about her dog was on *The New York Times* bestseller list for 29 weeks.

In Europe, the greyhound breed was first used by 9th century aristocrats to hunt such small game as hares. Several hundred years later, the greyhound was featured prominently in such famous Renaissance tapestries as "The Hunt of the Unicorn."

Each day in the United States, animal shelters destroy 30,000 dogs and cats.

The chow is the only breed of dog with a black tongue and black gums. Its tongue and gums start out pink but turn completely dark by the eighth week.

The chow's heavy head and muzzle is surrounded by an off-standing ruff, a little like a lion. Its eyes are almond shaped and deep set, giving it an inscrutable, mysterious look.

Chows were bred in China about 3,000 years ago both for hunting and for food. Their thick fur was also shorn and woven into blankets to keep people warm.

Some researchers believe that the chow came first from the Arctic Circle and only later migrated to Mongolia, Siberia, and China.

The Canary Islands were named after a breed of large, wild dogs. The Latin name was *Canariae insulae*—"Island of Dogs."

Heart-attack patients who own dogs have a better than average chance of survival. The dog will react to the attack and alert others in the house or even those outside. This advantage does not apply to cat-owners.

GOLDEN EVOLUTION

The golden retriever breed of dog was "invented" in 19th century Scotland by an aristocrat. Sir Dudley Majoribanks, later Lord Tweedmouth, mated a flat coat retriever with an English water dog (now extinct). Four pups were born and used to begin a meticulous crossbreed program that covered 20 years and included such breeds as Labrador retrievers, flat coat retrievers, Irish setters, Tweed water spaniels, and even bloodhounds. The final result was our modern golden retriever.

German shepherds bite humans more often than any other breed of dog does.

Female dogs bite people twice as often as do male dogs.

A dog bite is less likely to cause infection than is a human bite.

The owners of aggressive-breed dogs like rottweilers, malamutes, Dobermans, akidas, Great Danes, and pit bulls are finding it increasingly difficult to obtain homeowner insurance policies.

Dogs have about 100 different facial expressions, most of them involving their ears. Due to breeding, some of the more aggressive dogs, like bulldogs and pit bulls, have only 10 expressions. This can lead to more fights with other dogs since aggressive dog signals can be misinterpreted.

SELECTIVE SMELLING

A dog is capable of distinguishing many individual odors in a complex smell. That pot of stew on the stove may smell wonderful to you, but your dog also gets to enjoy the scent of cooking meat, peas, carrots, onions, potatoes, and spices.

The Maui Grown Market convenience store in Hawaii offers souvenirs, snacks, drinks, suntan lotion, and a dog you can rent for the day from the owner's family of eleven.

Dogs with wrinkled faces, such as the bassett hound, are prone to two diseases of the eyelid called entropion and ectropion. Entropion causes the eyelid to curl up into itself; ectropion means the eyelid turns inside-out. With either condition, the eyelid no longer protects the eyeball, and the corneal scratches that can result from surrounding hairs and dust particles can cause the dog extreme pain.

Because of their large heads, bulldog puppies are often delivered by Caesarean section.

Two of the survivors from the Titanic were dogs, both belonging to wealthy passengers. Miss Margaret Hays of New York survived with her Pomeranian, and Henry Harper of the publishing family survived with his Pekinese.

The Irish wolfhound is one of the strongest dogs and can pick up another dog as large and heavy as a mastiff. When a wolfhound fights with another dog, it picks it up by the back and violently shakes it, breaking its neck.

In ancient Egypt, dogs were used in hunting, as guards and police reinforcements, in military actions, and were also enjoyed as household pets.

The ancient Egyptian word for dog was "iwiw," which imitated the sound of a dog's bark.

The basenji is the only breed that can't bark. Dogs that resemble this breed are shown in ancient Egyptian paintings.

Archeologists working in Egypt discovered the leather collars of domesticated dogs. Some collars had names inscribed such as "Brave One," "Excellent Herdsman," "Antelope Hunter," and even "Useless."

Your dog recognizes you by the scent of your feet!

A dog sees smiling as a sign of aggression. The smile reveals the teeth, indicating a possible attack.

Although the precise reason dogs eat grass is unknown, scientists believe the juices soothe a dog's irritated stomach and help digestion.

The Rhodesian ridgebacks are aptly named. A prominent line of forward-growing hairs can be seen along the tops of their backs.

If you own a dog for an average of 12 years, you will spend about $14,000 to take care of it.

The Great Pyrenees breed of dog is so sensitive to anesthesia that even a small amount can lead to cardiac arrest. Veterinarians performing surgery on them must be extra cautious.

Dalmatians are born pure white. The spots begin to develop in 6 to 8 weeks.

A Newfoundland dog is an excellent swimmer. The reason? Webbed feet!

A basset hound is a poor swimmer because its legs are too short to keep its long, heavy body afloat.

The "blood" in "bloodhound" refers to the dog's association with English aristocrats of noble bloodlines.

The name for the boxer breed of dog comes from its tendency to stand on its hind legs and "box" with its front paws when fighting.

The Arctic fox is a close relative of the red fox that also lives in the Arctic regions of Europe, Asia, and North America.

Young Arctic foxes are cared for by both parents—unusual in the canine world.

Unlike some Arctic mammals, Arctic foxes do not hibernate and can withstand temperatures as low as minus 122 degrees Fahrenheit (minus 50 degrees Celsius).

Arctic foxes are pure white in winter and brown in summer. They can also be light brown, gray, or black with a bluish hue in summer.

Coyotes are spread across Alaska, Canada, the continental United States, Mexico, and Central America.

Coyotes feed mostly on small mammals, but they also enjoy fruit, insects, frogs, snakes and—when available—crustaceans!

According to North American Indian lore, the coyote was the leader of all creatures in the pre-human animal age.

Coyotes only live about 8 years in the wild, 15 years in captivity.

Unlike many other canines, coyotes don't always live in packs, but hunt alone or in pairs. However, they live in dens that they come back to year after year.

Like domestic dogs, coyotes mark their territory with urine and by howling.

The coyote is one of the fastest runners of the dog family, and can reach speeds up to 37 miles (60km) per hour.

The coyote has a wide sound vocabulary with over 50 squeaks, howls, and yelps.

Coyotes are not endangered. Their population has actually increased, despite hunting by man.

The Australian wild dog or *dingo* originated from Asian wolves, which arrived in Australia with Asian seafarers about 4,000 years ago. Because of widespread interbreeding with domestic dogs, there are very few pure dingoes left.

If the dingo has a tail (some don't), it usually has a white tip at the end.

Dingoes are solitary animals, but often live in loosely knit groups. They also hunt in groups, especially when large prey is abundant.

THE DWINDLING GRAY WOLF

The gray wolf once had the largest distribution of any mammal except human beings. It was found throughout much of Eurasia, from the Arctic to the Mediterranean. In North America, it roamed from Alaska to the Sierra Madre in Mexico. Today, the gray wolf is found only in Canada, two northern U.S. states, Russia, and pockets of Eastern Europe. It has disappeared entirely from Western Europe.

There are several subspecies of the gray wolf, including the timber wolf, the Rocky Mountain wolf, the Arctic wolf, the Mexican wolf, the Japanese wolf, and the Indian wolf.

Gray wolves live in hierarchical packs containing anywhere from five to ten animals. The more food available, the larger the pack.

Because they are livestock predators, gray wolves have been trapped and killed by human hunters. Habitat encroachment by humans has also caused their numbers to dwindle. They are also extremely vulnerable to diseases spread by domestic dogs.

The alpha, or "boss" members of a gray wolf pack are always the first to eat.

About half the alpha members of packs are females.

Only the strongest and most aggressive within a pack will breed, usually in January.

Golden jackals are found in northern Africa and on the Balkan peninsula. Their population is only half of what it was 50 years ago.

Jackals are scavengers and will often follow lions and other big cats to eat what is discarded or dropped.

Jackals form lifetime bonds with their mates, but also hunt and socialize in larger packs.

The New Guinea singing dog makes an odd, bird-like sound unlike any other canid. It is the descendant of domestic dogs that reverted back to the wild in the early stages of domestication. These animals were discovered in 1957, when the first pair was brought down from the New Guinea Highlands to the Taronga Zoo in Sydney, Australia.

Singing dogs live in mountain forests and can exist at elevations above 6500 feet (2,000m). Because they are such successful game predators, singing dogs are hunted and killed by humans and are endangered in the wild.

Singing dogs make difficult pets because they can be tamed but not domesticated. Since they are such efficient predators, any small animal—including another small dog—is considered prey. This is not the case with domestic dogs, which tend not to fight with dogs smaller than themselves.

Singing dogs are not pack animals and consider any dog—even one of its own type—a rival for territory and mates. This means that fights between male dogs are common.

Even friendly singing dogs can "get into trouble" with other dogs because their mode of play differs from that of domestic dogs. Singing dogs display less "play initiation," such as bowing down on forepaws, and will abruptly jump an unsuspecting playmate.

Also called the tree fox, because it climbs trees to escape from predators, the gray fox lives in the southwestern United States and Mexico.

Gray foxes prefer a den made from a hollow tree. Failing that, they'll make a burrow next to a rock or tree stump.

Gray foxes take a mate for life and usually hunt with their mates or cubs.

Gray foxes have crepuscular vision, which means that their vision is best at dawn or dusk, their most active hunting times.

Having the body of a dog and the striped face of a raccoon, the curious raccoon dog was once so widely hunted in Asia that only a few hundred were left.

The raccoon dog is not related to the raccoon.

Raccoon dogs are excellent swimmers and enjoy eating frogs and fish. They also feed on rodents, fruits, berries, nuts, and carrion.

Until recently, about 70,000 raccoon dogs were killed every year in Japan for their fur and for folk medicine preparations.

To protect raccoon dogs against extinction, a small island off the coast of Japan has now been designated a protected area for the animals.

We have much to learn about the graceful birds that soar in lazy circles above us. But we also have a few things to learn about the ostrich, turkey, and some other feathered wobblers who can hardly walk—much less fly—gracefully. Have fun discovering some unfamiliar facts about familiar winged creatures.

Worldwide, there are over 9,200 species of birds. These species exist in a wide variety of habitats, from tropical to polar.

All birds have feathers, and only birds have feathers.

A bird plucked of its feathers can't fly.

Most birds don't have a very good sense of taste or smell. But chickens like sweets and pigeons seem to prefer salty food.

A bird's eyes can focus very quickly. This allows it to fly through dense trees without crashing into the branches.

In the United States alone, over 1,000 birds a year die from smashing into windows.

Bird droppings are the chief export of Nauru, an island nation in the western Pacific. The droppings are high in nitrogen and make excellent fertilizer. Birds cannot urinate. Their droppings contain urine in the form of urates, the whitish-green portion of their droppings.

Pet birds that live in homes with cigarette, cigar, or pipe smoke can develop serious eye problems, skin irritations, and respiratory diseases. Most birds recover if the source of the smoke is removed.

Many household cleaning agents and disinfectants can poison pet birds. Chlorine bleach and ammonia contain vapors that can quickly suffocate even large birds, like parrots.

Aerosol products—perfume, deodorant, hairspray — used around pet birds can cause the linings of their lungs to become inflamed.

A chemical in chocolate, *theobromide*, is poisonous to many species of birds, including parrots. The skins and pits of avocados are also dangerous.

Your house is dangerous to a bird out of its cage. Large, curious birds can electrocute themselves by chewing through electric cords. Smaller birds can explore hidden places where they can get hurt.

Small birds sometimes like to "nest" in piles of dirty laundry. This creates the obvious danger of throwing your bird in with the wash!

Cat bites can be fatal to a bird, even if the wound is not serious. Cat saliva contains the *Pasteurella* bacteria, which can lead to fatal blood poisoning.

Salty foods—crackers and chips—if eaten in sufficient quantities may be toxic to birds.

HOLD THE ONIONS

Although onions can cause fatal hemolytic anemia in dogs and cats, the red blood cells of birds appear to protect them from onion toxicity. But it's still not a good idea to put onions in your bird's feed!

It's not a good idea to let your bird kiss you—the bacteria and fungi in your mouth are far more dangerous to your pet than any bug your pet might give you.

Scientists know much more about the history and evolution of mammals and reptiles than they know about birds. This is because birds have very fragile bones that do not fossilize as easily as bones of mammals and reptiles.

The hollow bones of a pigeon weigh less than its feathers.

Scientists believe that birds evolved from small meat-eating dinosaurs around 150 million years ago. The earliest known bird is *Archaeopteryx lithographica,* whose fossil was found in 145-million-year-old limestone in southern Germany.

Diatryma were heavy-built, flightless birds that date from 38 million to 2 million years ago. They were about seven feet (2.1m) tall, had thick legs with clawed feet, tiny wings, and huge, powerful, hooked beaks on a big head.

The earliest bird fossils found in Australia are 110 million years old and from a site called Lightning Ridge. The fossils are preserved in solid opal!

Scientist believe that the earlist true birds, including *Archaeopteryx*, flew clumsily and may have had to take off from trees or cliffs.

Possibly the largest bird that ever lived, the *Dromornis stirtoni*, lived in Australia 15 million years ago and weighed as much as 992 pounds (450kg).

The design of a bird's body is optimized for flight. Its bones are hollow and thin-walled to reduce weight, and many internal organs are reduced in size. In fact, most of the organs you find in pairs in other vertebrates, such as kidneys, are reduced to one in birds.

An ostrich sticks its head in the sand to search for water.

The ostrich yolk is the largest single cell in the world.

Six people can feast on one ostrich egg for breakfast.

Most talking parrots have a vocabulary of about 20 words.

Mockingbirds imitate any sound from a squeaking door to a meowing cat. In urban areas, they can even mimic car alarms and cell phone rings.

Feeding hens certain dyes causes the yolks of their eggs to take on the color of the dye.

The hummingbird, nature's smallest bird, weighs only 0.14 ounces (4g), and is so tiny that one of its predators is an insect—the praying mantis.

Hummingbirds eat more insects than nectar. Ants are their favorite insect meal.

Adding red dye to your hummingbird feeder solution makes no difference to the hummingbird. The bird is really more attracted to the little flower ornament on the tip of the feeding tube—and its shape—than to any color in the liquid.

The hummingbird is the only bird that can fly backwards.

A hummingbird's heart beats 1,260 times per minute.

Flamingoes lay their eggs on top of volcano-shaped nests made of mud.

Only male turkeys (toms) gobble; females make a clicking noise.

Turkeys will peck to death members of the flock that are physically inferior or different.

Penguins can jump as high as six feet (1.83m) in the air.

The penguin is the only bird that can swim but cannot fly.

In Miami, Florida, roosting vultures have taken to snatching poodles from rooftop patios.

Starlings will attack pedestrians and bicyclists who come too close to their nests.

In the 19th century, miners would often use a live caged canary to test for toxic fumes in an old mine. The bird was placed in the cave. If it died, the miners knew fumes were present and they had to stay out.

Unlike humans, canaries can regenerate their brain cells.

Birds can show an approaching outbreak of West Nile virus in the human population. Certain species, like crows, ravens, and jays, will die of the virus about 50 days prior to the first reports of human infection.

An eagle can kill a young deer and fly away with it.

A group of geese on the ground is a gaggle; a group of geese in the air is a skein.

Pelicans can work as a team for fishing. A line of pelicans will form near a school of fish, and then close the line into a circle, trapping the fish.

The pouch under a pelican's bill holds up to 25 pounds (11.3kg) of fish and water.

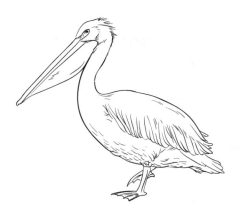

The pelican is the only bird that can use its baggy beak as a "net" to catch fish.

Adult pelicans will often form "babysitting" groups to tend to young pelicans when their parents are away.

The bird we call a peacock should actually be called a peafowl—the male is a peacock and the female a peahen. It is a large pheasant that lives in the Indian subcontinent. It seldom flies, but runs from danger.

How fast can a woodpecker peck? Twenty times a second.

The feathers of a blue jay are actually gray. The blue color is caused by light reflecting from the surface of the feathers.

The shape of a bird's beak evolved according to the kind of food it liked to eat. For example, short-sharp-beaked birds prefer seeds, while blade-beaked birds enjoy insects or small mammals. Tubular beaks are for nectar-loving birds, like hummingbirds.

Birds do not like safflower seeds and will often spit them out if they accidentally bite into one.

GROUNDED DUE TO HIGH WINDS

Contrary to popular belief, high winds do not carry small birds long distances against their will. Although a large bird will sometimes use the wind to give it extra lift and speed, smaller birds will stay grounded because of the danger of uncontrolled flight. If a wind should pick up a small bird, it almost always refuses to fly and lets itself drop to the ground.

Scientists still can't explain why some birds stray dramatically from their expected migration routes. Some theorize that it might have to do with variations in Earth's magnetic field.

Some species of migrating birds, like the cranes, can fly nonstop for several days and nights and cover a distance as great as 7,000 miles (11,265km).

Birds build their nests everywhere, from directly on the ground to the tops of trees. The Belted Kingfisher builds its nest in the bank of a river or a creek, digging it 4 feet (1.21m) deep into the bank. Grebes build a floating nest on water. Understanding that birds place their nests everywhere is important for protecting birds during the nesting season.

AN OLD MYTH DEBUNKED

It's not true that if you touch a bird's nest, the parent bird will not return to its young. Scientists have conducted thousands of studies that involved touching, weighing, and photographing bird nests, and in practically all cases, the parent bird returned once she felt no threat. The origin of the abandoned nest rumor probably has to do with how human scent can disrupt where birds choose to nest. It's not that your smell offends the birds, but that they sense that mammal predators will follow a human scent looking for food. So it's not about you, but about that squirrel you might attract.

The V formation of flocking birds allows the flock to use less energy when it covers long distances. It allows birds in the rear to glide on the airstreams of the birds ahead. The formation also allows birds to communicate more effectively, both aurally and visually.

Bird blood is similar to human blood in that it contains white cells for fighting infection, platelets for clotting, and red cells for carrying oxygen. But bird blood cells contain a nucleus.

The red blood cells of birds have about 20 times as much oxygen-carrying hemoglobin as the red blood cells of humans. This is because flying takes a tremendous amount of energy, and energy requires oxygen consumption.

A bird's heart is similar to a human's in that it has four chambers and four valves. But a bird's heart beats much faster than ours and pumps much more blood for its size.

The wings of birds have the basic bone structure of human arms. Both wings and arms have the same ulna, radius, and metacarpal bones.

Most perching birds have three or four toes, with one toe pointing backwards. But some birds, such as cuckoos, owls, and parrots, clutch with two toes forward and two back. Zoologists call these groups *zygodactylus* (meaning two-of-the-same toes).

The voice box of humans is called the *larynx*. The voice box of birds is called the *syrinx*.

Birds have a higher body temperature than humans. They average 106 degrees Fahrenheit (41 degrees Celsius) to our 98.6 degrees Fahrenheit (37 degrees Celsius.)

A bird's ears are located right behind its eyes. The ears are flat holes covered by a certain kind of feather that protects them from wind when the bird is flying.

Birds of prey like the eagle and falcon have eyesight eight times sharper than human eyesight.

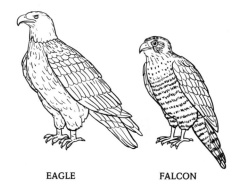

EAGLE   FALCON

Bird's eyes are placed on opposite sides of their heads, which means that they can detect motion on both sides of their bodies at once.

The bird with the longest feathers is the Onagadori, or Red Jungle Fowl. Its tail can reach a length of 34.75 feet (10m).

Unlike most birds, owls have eyes that face forward. This allows them to have binocular (three-dimensional) vision—helpful in judging distances.

Owls are one of the few birds that can see the color blue.

On an owl, the ear hole on the left side of its head is in a different place than the ear hole on the right side. This creates a slight time lag when a sound wave moves from the left to the right ear and helps the owl more accurately figure out the location of its prey.

Birds only half-sleep. One half of their brain remains alert and the other half sleeps. The eye controlled by the sleeping half shuts and the other stays open and watchful.

BIRD WINDSHIELD?

Unlike humans, many birds—especially the fast-flying, diving ones—have a special third eyelid that protects their eyes from the wind. Called a "nictitating membrane," this third eyelid allows the bird to keep its eyes safe while flying at high speeds or diving into water. Although the eyelid isn't completely transparent, it allows enough light to pass through so that the bird can keep to a steady course.

The snipe has eyes so close to the top of its head that it can look straight up without moving its head.

The yellow-tailed black cockatoo will sit for hours in a tree pressing one of its ear holes against the bark. It's listening for the sound of insects. Suddenly the cockatoo will rip away a strip of bark and enjoy a feast!

The short, inwardly curved beak of the parrot is designed for cracking hard seeds or nuts.

Birds that love nectar, like hummingbirds, have long narrow bills that can reach into the center of blossoms.

Sand-digging birds, like the egret, have long, shovel-shaped bills that help them uncover small crabs.

Ducks and swans don't feed their young. They just guide them to food.

Most birds can store food under their beaks—either for eating later or to carry back to their young. The food is stored in a sac called a "crop," located in the lower end of the neck.

Because a bird doesn't have teeth, the bird's gizzard helps its stomach grind and digest food. Some birds, like the emu, actually swallow stones to help their gizzards do the job.

Meat-eating birds like the hawk can't digest the bones, teeth, fur, or feathers of their prey. Instead, their gizzards grind these materials into small pellets that the hawk can regurgitate later.

Flesh-eating birds like eagles, hawks, and owls all have sharp hooks at the end of their bills to help them tear the flesh from their prey.

Birds born without any feathery covering at all (like sparrows) are called "altricial." Birds born with a downy protective covering (like chicks and ducklings) are called "precocial." The covered birds can be led straight to water and shown how to find food. The uncovered birds must wait until they're stronger.

When a flock of birds is snoozing together, the birds on the outer edges of the flock keep one eye open—the eye that looks to the outside. They're literally guarding the flock!

A sleeping bird won't fall off its perch because its toes lock into place when its legs are bent. An alert bird straightens its legs, unlocking its toes.

A raptor (a bird of prey) can't unlock its toes from the animal it's carrying until it lands.

The frigatebird eats and drinks only when flying. It drinks saltwater, but de-salts it through special glands located just above its eyes. The fresh water is swallowed and the salty brine is excreted through their nostrils.

Not all birds build their own nests! Some, like the cuckoo, are called "brood parasites" because they put their eggs in the nests of other birds.

The water-diving gannet dives so steeply that its skull is reinforced to absorb the shock of impact. The gannet also has an air sac under the skin of its chest to cushion the shock.

THE BUILT-IN COMPASS OF A BIRD

Birds have specialized otolith organs in their inner ears that contain traces of magnetized iron. These organs help birds sense the magnetic north pole, and are useful for navigation. Studies conducted by Hiroshima University professor Yasuo Harada found that the otolith organs of various species of birds could contain from 0.7 to 4.3 percent iron.

The brain of a bird can actually increase in size when extra neurons are needed. For example, the vocal center of the brain enlarges each spring when a bird composes new birdsongs.

The *hyperstriatum* area of the brain in birds is extremely well developed. This is the area used for learning and remembering surroundings for navigation.

A NATURAL PESTICIDE

Birds will sometimes shuffle on an anthill to bring out the ants. Then they'll pick up the ants and place them in their feathers. The disturbed ants secrete formic acid that rids the birds of lice and other parasites.

Even though scientists have studied the behavior of homing pigeons for well over 100 years, they still don't understand how these amazing birds manage to find their way back to their starting places.

You can take a healthy homing pigeon 500 miles (805km) from its loft and release it, and it will return home in 24 hours—even if blindfolded.

A human-reared bird will happily share food, space, and playthings with a bird of another species, if introduced to it by the human.

Birds that have lived with humans show increased individuality, such as different likes and dislikes in food. This quality is called "conspecificity."

Terns, relatives of the seagull, take care of each other. It's not unusual to see an injured tern lifted to safety by two companions, each supporting a wing.

Injured birds reared by humans and then freed will sometimes call on the human to follow them to the site of other fallen nestlings.

A bird sometimes remains on the ground near a fallen mate, pushing its companion as if trying to wake it.

It is hard to believe, but herons and egrets actually nest in the tops of tall trees on the California mainland. Nesting in trees is a good strategy for protection against predators, but a challenge for large, top-heavy birds with very long legs.

Herons and egrets pull their necks in when they fly. Spoonbills, ibis, and swans always fly with their necks stretched out.

Certain birds, like the Australian bowerbird, enjoy decorating their nests or cages with colorful objects. Bowerbirds will spend hours rearranging things until their environment is just right!

THE MYSTERY OF FLOCKING BEHAVIOR

Flocking is not a quality of any individual bird but emerges only as a property of a group of birds. Each bird acts independently and instinctively follows a simple set of flocking rules:

- Separation to avoid crashing into flock mates.
- Alignment with the general navigational direction of flock mates.
- Adaptation to changes in flock direction due to wind or other obstacles.

These rules were first identified and simulated in a computer model by programmer Craig Reynolds in the 1980s.

Pelicans flying in flocks will actually synchronize their wing beats to those of the leading bird. This reduces work by maximizing the airstream efficiency, allowing the entire flock to glide more.

Our ancestors are still among us in the form of anglerfish, cephalopods, and nematodes. Swimming things come in all shapes, sizes, colors, and even flavors. Read more about some strange animals that lurk underwater.

105

Nine out of every ten living things dwell in the ocean.

A lobster can lay up to 150,000 eggs at one time.

More than 20,000,000 seahorses are harvested each year for folk medicinal purposes.

The world seahorse population has dropped 70 percent in the past ten years.

More types of fish swim in Brazil's Amazon River than in the entire Atlantic Ocean.

Tuna swim an average of nine miles (14.5km) per hour, constantly. They never stop moving.

Starfish have multiple eyes—one at the end of each "leg" (starfish can have from five to eight legs).

The starfish is one of the only animals that can turn its stomach inside out.

Starfish have no brain; neither do jellyfish.

A jellyfish is 95 percent water!

The catfish has over 30,000 taste buds. That makes it rank #1 among fish for taste-sensitivity.

A shrimp's heart is located in its head.

The tongue of a blue whale weighs more than most elephants.

Dolphins sleep with one eye open.

The Mola mola, or ocean sunfish, lays up to 5,000,000 eggs at a time.

Discovered in 1990, the round goby has reproduced so quickly that it may completely replace native fish in the Great Lakes by 2010!

Most freshwater eels migrate to salt water to spawn.

Sturgeon live in salt water but migrate to freshwater to spawn.

Only one in 100 salmon eggs will survive to hatch. The rest will be eaten by predators.

The flapping fins of the hatchetfish can propel it out of the water to glide for up to 20 feet (6m).

The most common name for pet goldfish? Jaws.

A 400-million-year-old fish, the coelacanth ("see-la-kanth"), once thought to be extinct, is still living today.

The first coelecanth to be rediscovered was found by Marjorie Courtenay Latimer, curator of a tiny museum in South Africa, on the deck of a ship she was visiting. She took the five-foot specimen back to the museum in a taxi!

In 1984, live fish fell on a London neighborhood, startling residents. The fish had been sucked up in a waterspout about an hour earlier.

The Australian lungfish forms cocoons in the muddy bottoms of outback swamps. When the swamps dry up and the outback returns to its desert climate, the lungfish hibernates until the next rainfall.

Flying fish evolved the ability to leap out of the water and sail in the air as a way of eluding predators.

There are 20,000 known species of fish. Scientists estimate that there may be as many as 20,000 more species yet to be discovered.

The most primitive types of fish, like lampreys and hagfishes, have sucking mouths. For these fish, evolution stopped before they could develop biting jaws.

The whale shark is the world's largest fish—growing to about 50 feet (15m) in length and weighing several tons.

The basking shark is the next largest shark. It is also called the sunfish, the bone shark, the elephant shark, the sailfish shark, and the big-mouth shark.

The most abundant fish in the sea is any of the several species of *cyclothone*, a deepwater fish sometimes called "bristle mouth." The fish is about three inches (7.6cm) long and swims at a depth of around 1,640 feet (500m).

Fish that give birth to living young are called viviparous. These include sharks and sea perches of the Pacific, whose young can be nearly one-quarter the size of their mother.

LIFE UNDER PRESSURE

Fish are found at virtually all depths. In 1960, scientists aboard the bathyscape Trieste discovered a flatfish happily swimming at a depth of 35,800 feet (10,912m). As recently as 1930, scientists believed that life was impossible below a depth of 1,800 feet (549m).

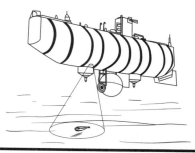

Anadromous refers to fish that are born in freshwater, spend most of their lives in the sea, then return to freshwater to spawn. Salmon, smelt, shad, striped bass, and sturgeon are all examples of anadromous fish.

A *diadromous* fish migrates between freshwater and saltwater. The migration patterns differ for each species and have seasonal and lifecycle variations. Only one percent of all fish in the world are diadromous. There are five species of diadromous Pacific salmon.

A *catadromous* fish lives in freshwater but migrates into salt water to spawn. Most eels are catadromous.

**WHAT DO FISH AND
TREES HAVE IN COMMON?**

Scientists can determine the age of a fish by counting ringlike structures found on the otoliths, or small bones of the inner ear. The rings correspond to seasonal changes in the environment and can be compared with the annual rings of tree trunks.

Most fish have a life span of 10 to 20 years in temperate waters. Small reef fishes live only a few weeks or months, while the sturgeon can live to 50 years. The longest living fish is the saltwater rougheye rockfish, which lives to be 150 years old.

Fresh fish are odorless. Fish begin to smell "fishy" when decay sets in. This is often caused by faulty storage practices that bring about the release of oxidized fats and acids through bacterial and enzymatic action.

HOW DO FISH BREATHE?

Fish "breathe" by taking oxygen from the water. As water passes over a system of fine gill membranes, a network of fine blood vessels called capillaries absorbs the oxygen and passes it into the bloodstream.

Fish "swim" by contracting bands of muscles in sequence on alternate sides of their body so that the tail is whipped very rapidly from side to side in a motion called "sculling."

Although most fish can swim backwards, they seldom do it unless caught in a small space. Backward, or blind, swimming prevents a fish from seeing predators or food sources. However, eels seem comfortable swimming backwards.

Most fish swim horizontally. The exceptions are the seahorses and shrimpfish of the Indian Ocean, which swim with their long tube-like snouts pointing directly upward. Catfish native to the Nile and other African rivers also swim vertically.

Fish can't chew, since chewing would cause them to suffocate. Most carnivorous species of fish have sharp or hammerlike teeth that can rip prey into smaller pieces before it is swallowed.

Herbivorous fish often lack teeth but have tooth-like grinding mills in their throats, called pharyngeal teeth.

Indigestion can be dangerous for a fish. The buildup of gasses inside its body can cause it to float to the surface where it can be eaten by birds.

Most fish are colorblind. They can see shades of grey, reflected light, shape, and movement, which probably accounts for their indifference to colorful artificial lures used by fishermen.

Sardines travel in schools that may contain hundreds of thousands to millions of individuals. The large numbers of fish in the schools and their rapid coordinated movements serve to protect them from predators. They are migratory and may travel more than 600 miles (1000km) between feeding and spawning habitats over the course of a year.

Herring form the food base for many larger species of fish because the primary diet of herring is a microscopic animal called zooplankton. Since they are the primary converters of plankton, herring play a vital role in the food chain.

"Pearl essence," the silvery substance in the skin of herring-like fishes, is used in the manufacture of lipstick, nail polish, paints, and ceramics.

FISH USED FOR CHICKEN FEED

With flesh too oily and strong-tasting for human consumption, the Atlantic menhaden fish still provides important ingredients for other industries. Meal made from the manhaden improves the growth rates of poultry, swine, and cattle. The oil of the menhaden is rich in nutrious Omega 3 fatty acids, which are added to sauces, salad dressings, sports drinks—even baked goods!

Tuna have scales, but the scales are so small that they're practically invisible. Prominent scaling appears only around the head and cheeks, and in a triangular area near the gills.

A fish that has both eyes on the left side of its body is called sinistral. A fish that has both eyes on the right side of its body is called dextral. Turbots and other flatfish are sinistral or dextral.

All four species of sunfish can grow between seven and ten feet (2.1 and 3m) in length. The biggest sunfish catch ever recorded weighed 3,102 pounds (1,407kg).

Porcupine and other puffer fish inflate themselves by pumping water into special sacs. They do this to appear larger and scare off predators. When a porcupine fish is taken out of water, it fills its sacs with air.

The average discharge of an electric eel is about 350 volts, but discharges as high as 650 volts have been measured.

Most eels have embedded scales. You can't see them, but you can feel them if you stroke against the direction of their growth.

A newborn moray eel is almost completely transparent and practically invisible.

Sharks have no air bladders, so they must swim constantly or they'll sink.

The deeper the water a shark lives in, the wider and more sensitive its eyes.

The blue color of the blue shark quickly fades to gray once the animal dies.

Shark "bones" are actually made of cartilage, the grainy stuff that your ears and nose are made of. However, as sharks age, calcium salts deposit in their skeletal cartilage and strengthen it.

SHARK ATTRACTORS

Scientists are undecided about what attracts sharks, but certain types of irregular sounds, like those made by a swimmer in trouble or a damaged fish, can bring them closer. In fact, many scientists now believe that hearing, rather than sight or smell, is the primary sense the shark uses for hunting.

Studies suggest that sharks can distinguish light colors from dark ones and that they might even be able to distinguish colors. They seem most responsive to yellow, white, red, and silver. Many divers suggest that clothing, fins, and tanks should be painted in dull colors to avoid attracting sharks.

Based on the number of recorded shark attacks, the most dangerous sharks are the great white shark, bull shark, tiger shark, gray nurse shark, lemon shark, blue shark, hammerhead shark, and mako shark.

GREAT WHITE SHARK

BULL SHARK

TIGER SHARK

GRAY NURSE SHARK

LEMON SHARK

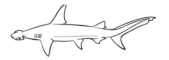

BLUE SHARK

HAMMERHEAD SHARK

MAKO SHARK

Sharks can survive 6 weeks without feeding. The record fast was 15 months for a swell shark of the Indian Ocean.

Sharks are omnivorous, which means they eat both meat and vegetation. But they prefer meat and consume vegetation only when meat is scarce.

The largest shark—the whale shark—is mainly a plankton feeder.

Sharks have taste buds in the mouth, not on the tongue, as we have.

A shark's sense of smell is directional. Its twin nasal cavities work like two ears. Odor coming from the left of the shark arrives at the left cavity just before it arrives at the right cavity. This allows the shark to figure out where the smell is coming from.

DO SHARKS HAVE ESP?

Sharks have three senses that humans do not. One of these is the ability to detect electricity. A network of cells on the skin near their heads—called the ampullae of Lorenzini—detects weak electric fields generated by the muscle contractions of other animals. These cells can also detect Earth's magnetic field and so help the shark navigate.

Another sensory organ of the shark allows it to detect the slightest vibration in the water, such as that of an injured fish. Called the "lateral line system," it consists of two long tubes that run along the top of the shark's body. These tubes, flushed with water as the shark swims, are lined with pressure-sensing cells.

Third, sharks have "pit organs" in their heads that scientists believe aid them in detecting infrared light or tiny temperature variations in the water.

A shark "test bites" a potential meal before consuming it. The taste buds clustered around the front of the shark's mouth analyze the food to see if it's palatable. Unless very hungry, sharks will reject prey—such as humans—that fall outside their normal diet.

Spawning salmon return to the precise stream of their birth, sometimes traveling great distances and overcoming hazardous river conditions to reach home. Scientists still don't understand their exact method of navigation.

Depending on the species, salmon will lay from 2,500 to 7,000 eggs. The Chinook salmon generally produces the most and largest eggs.

Octopus and squid are *cephalopods*, which have developed hiding to a fine art. They swim by jet propulsion and can change color in a split second using pigment cells called *chromatophores*. Their survival depends on it!

At 60 feet (18m) long, the giant squid is the biggest cephalopod. It has ten arms and its eyes are the size of basketballs.

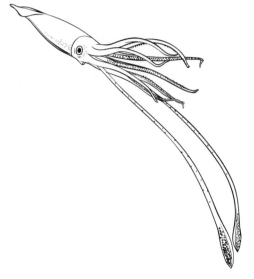

Fewer than 50 giant squids have been spotted in the past century.

LOBSTERS ON THE LAM

Lobsters living near the shore tend to stay in one place, rarely straying more than a mile or two away. Deepwater lobsters follow a seasonal migratory pattern—moving towards the shore in summer and returning to deep water in the autumn. A tagged lobster was recorded traveling a distance of 225 miles (362km)—the world record.

A lobster's blood is colorless, but when exposed to the air, it develops a bluish tint.

A lobster can survive about four days out of water if kept in a cool, moist environment.

A lobster begins the molting process by absorbing excess water into its body so that it can literally break out of its own shell. Molting occurs about 25 times in the first five to seven years of a lobster's life.

A lobster molts about 30 times before it reaches the market size of one pound (0.45kg). This can take up to seven years!

Lobsters come in a variety of colors, with blue, yellow, greenish-brown, and orange the more frequent hues. They can also have spotted or blotchy patterns.

A COOKED LOBSTER TURNS RED

Cooking a lobster appears to turn it red, but what actually happens is that the cooking destroys other pigments in the lobster shell—such as the greens and browns—that hide the red color.

After molting, lobsters eat their discarded shells. This replaces the calcium lost during molting and speeds up the hardening of the new shell, which takes from 14 to 30 days to mature.

Lobsters are nocturnal. They do most of their moving and hunting during the night.

Lobsters can discard and then regenerate some of their body parts, such as claws, legs, and antennae. This is a handy feature when such a body part is grabbed by a predator or snared in a trap.

The teeth of a lobster are in its stomach. Food is actually "chewed" in the stomach by three grinding surfaces called "gastric mills."

A freshly laid lobster egg is about the size of a pinhead.

A one-pound (0.45kg) female lobster carries about 8,000 eggs. A nine pound (4kg) female can carry over 100,000 eggs.

The female lobster carries eggs inside her body for the first 9 to 12 months. After this time, the eggs emerge under the fan-shaped parts of her tail, called the swimmerets. These exposed eggs—up to 150,000 of them—are now ready to be fertilized by a male lobster.

For every 50,000 eggs a lobster lays, only two will survive to become full-grown lobsters.

HARD AND SOFT CRABS

There is no difference between a soft-shell crab and a regular crab. A soft-shell crab is one that has just finished molting and has only a soft covering over its body. It will often bury itself in sand or mud to escape predators and emerge when its shell is fully hardened—in about a week.

A crab will increase about one-third its size each time it molts.

The "coconut crab" is a large, hermit land crab that lives on tropical Pacific islands. The crab gets its name because it eats coconuts that fall from trees and crack.

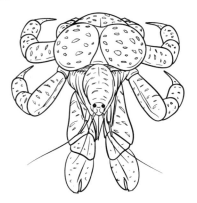

The Alaskan king crab is the largest crustacean, weighing up to 15 pounds (6.8kg) and measuring about 5 feet (1.5m) across shell and claws.

The biggest clam is the Tridacna, native to the Indian and Pacific Oceans. When fully grown, this clam can weigh nearly 500 pounds (227kg).

You can tell how old a clam is by counting the ridges on its shell. Each year, a clam expands its shell by depositing a thin layer of tissue at the inner and outer ridges.

Depending on the species, shrimp range in size from about a half inch (1.27cm) to almost 12 inches (30cm) long.

Depending on geography, some species of shrimp live as long as six and a half years. Others live only a year at most.

A shrimp produces around 500,000 eggs in a single spawning.

The holes at the edge of an abalone shell are actually vents for the animal's internal gills. Oxygenated water is regularly passed through the holes as part of the abalone's respiratory process.

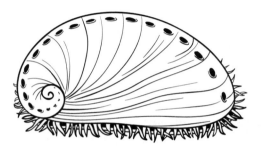

A scallop moves by forcing water backward through its shell hinge. The water jet drives the scallop in the direction of the shell opening.

Diarrheic Shellfish Poisoning (DSP) can affect those who consume shellfish containing microscopic algae. The toxin, okadiac acid, is not destroyed by cooking the shellfish.

Sewage-polluted shellfish, transplanted to clean water, purify themselves rapidly and become safe to eat.

Cooking will not destroy harmful viruses, like hepatitis, found in some shellfish.

A factory ship is a vessel designed to catch and process huge amounts of fish. In one hour, one factory ship can haul as much cod (about 100 tons) as a typical boat of the sixteenth century could land in three months.

Sea turtles nest in large groups called "*arribadas.*" Sea turtles living in particularly frigid seawater will sometimes wash ashore "cold-stunned" because their body temperature has dropped below normal. Lethargic and disoriented in this condition, the turtles are easy prey for predators.

With a shell that can reach 6 feet (1.8m) long and weigh 1,400 pounds (635kg), the leatherback is the largest sea turtle. Unlike most other species of sea turtle, the leatherback has rubbery skin instead of scales.

THE TRUTH ABOUT SAND DOLLARS

Sand dollars, those hollow white disks with vague star patterns you see at low tide, are not creatures at all. The sand dollar is the egg case made by moon snails. The snails lay their eggs in a gelatin-like mass, mixed with sand. The case hardens, protecting the eggs. When the eggs hatch, they escape through the hole in the sand dollar's center.

Whales, dolphins, and porpoises are mammals, just like humans. All are warm-blooded, breathe air, and bear living young, which are nursed by their mothers.

Jellyfish have been on earth for more than 650 million years.

Jellyfish take two basic forms: the anenome type that attaches to rocks and the free-floating medusa.

MEDUSA

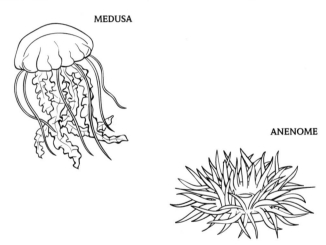

ANENOME

The venom in a jellyfish can remain active for weeks after the jellyfish dies.

The bioluminescent chemical found in jellyfish that allows them to glow in the dark has been used by doctors to trace the movement of specific chemicals through the human body.

Jellyfish have no brains, nerves, eyes, ears, or circulatory systems. They are one of the most primitive life forms in nature.

Most jellyfish live in shallow coastal waters, but some thrive in depths of nearly 12,000 feet (3,657m).

Jellyfish display a wide variety of sizes—from the 2-inch (5cm) diameter *Vellela vellela* of the Pacific, to the Arctic lion's mane jellyfish that can weigh a ton and have tentacles up to 100 feet (30m) long.

Jellyfish live no more than six months, with most having a life span of three months.

Jellyfish drift with the currents and have little control over horizontal movement. But because of the ring of muscles around their bell, they have a certain amount of vertical movement.

The real danger of a jellyfish sting is that the swimmer panics, exhausts himself, and drowns. In most cases, the sting itself poses no real danger to humans.

Placing alcohol on a jellyfish sting stimulates the venom and causes the sting to smart even more.

A humpback whale will sometimes construct a "bubble net" around a school of fish to trap them. The whale then lunges up through the bottom of the net to get its food.

A manatee's closest relative is the elephant. Some biologists believe the manatee is actually the descendant of an elephant that crawled back into the ocean 50 million years ago.

Seals, sea lions, and walruses are all called *pinnipeds*. This is a suborder of the order *Carnivora* which includes bears, dogs, otters, raccoons, and weasels.

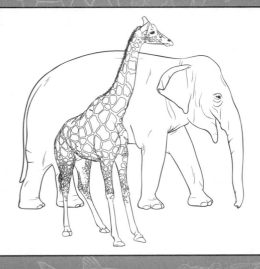

The jungles, savannahs, and tropical forests of the world are filled with some of the most spectacular creatures Nature has to offer. These familiar animals are endlessly fascinating—their sizes, colors, sounds, and strength all make them stunning reminders that the earth is an amazing place.

139

There are five species of rhinoceros found in Asia and Africa, but their numbers have decreased to only five percent of their population of 50 years ago.

Rhinos are part of the same family as horses and are thought to have inspired the myth of the unicorn.

Rhinos live only in areas that are no more than a day's trip from water.

The average life span of a rhino is 50 years.

African rhinos are more aggressive than their Asian counterparts and tend to be better fighters. Asian rhinos use their sharp bottom teeth to bite and tear at an enemy while African rhinos use their horns to butt and gore their enemies.

Both African and Asian rhinos actively graze throughout the night and early morning and spend most of the afternoon sleeping.

Rhinos can sleep both standing up and lying down.

Rhinos have a running walk, or canter, of about 45 miles (72km) an hour. However, they can only sustain this speed for a few minutes.

Rhinos use the bulk of their bodies to penetrate thick brush and leave a path behind for other rhinos to follow.

Among young male rhinos, groups of "bachelors" form. When a young male finds a mate, he leaves the group.

Paired rhinoceroses may stay together for up to four months before each finds another mate. Usually the male initiates the "breakup."

Rhinoceroses have been hunted to the point of near extinction because all parts of their bodies have been used as folk remedies. The most prized part of the rhino is the horn, which has been used as an aphrodisiac, fever-reducing drug, dagger, water finder, and as a potion for detecting poison.

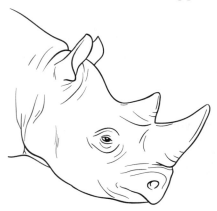

The largest land animals in the world are the African and Asian elephants, with the African elephant the larger of the two.

Elephants communicate using sounds between 14 and 35 hertz, well below the range of human hearing.

In captivity, African elephants reject the rough foliage and bark of their wild days and prefer to munch on hay, grain, and sweet vegetables. Carrots are a favorite!

Elephants walk on their toes because their soles are made up of boneless, fatty pads that flatten with each step. The sturdy toenails, located at the front of each foot, help support the elephant's weight.

An adult elephant consumes about six to eight percent of its body weight in vegetation each day.

A full-grown elephant will spend as many as 18 hours a day feeding.

Elephants prefer grass, tree foliage, bark, roots, shrubs, and fruit. They'll also eat soil for its mineral content.

Elephants digest only about 40 percent of what they eat.

A thirsty adult elephant can drink 26 gallons (100 liter) of water at one time. A very thirsty elephant can drink nearly 55 gallons (208 liter) in only a few minutes.

On average, an elephant lives 50 to 60 years.

An adult African elephant can weigh up to 15,500 pounds (7,045kg).

Between 1979 and 1989, Africa's elephant population dropped from 1,300,000 to about 700,000. This was due mostly to ivory hunting. Crackdowns on illegal ivory hunting have helped stabilize the elephant population since that time.

African elephants, which once lived throughout Africa, now inhabit only about a third of the continent.

An elephant has "fingers" at the end of its trunk that help it grasp things. The African elephant has two such fingers and the Asian elephant has one.

Anatomically speaking, the elephant's trunk is a combination of its upper lip and nose. It can grasp many things, including another elephant's tail. It's sensitive enough to pick up a single blade of grass and strong enough to move a large fallen tree.

The boneless trunk of an elephant is composed of about 40,000 muscles.

Elephants will sometimes use their trunks for snorkels, allowing them to breathe while crossing deep lakes and streams.

The average length of an elephant's trunk is 8 feet (2.4m).

Baby elephants suck their trunks, just as baby humans suck their thumbs.

Baby elephants have "milk tusks" that fall out after the elephant is about a year old.

The elephant's growth continues into old age, so seniors have the biggest tusks and do most of the breeding.

An elephant's tusks are actually elongated upper incisor teeth that grow throughout the elephant's life. The tusks are not always an exact match, and the larger tusk grows according to whether the elephant prefers its left or right side, just like a human's right or left handedness.

An average elephant's waistline is about 16 feet (4.9m).

After a 22-month pregnancy, a female elephant will produce a calf weighing about 200 pounds (90.7kg).

An adult elephant's heart weighs 48.5 pounds (22kg) and circulates about 119 gallons (450 liters) of blood, filtered by a 170 pound (77kg) liver.

An elephant releases about 528 gallons (2,000 liters) of methane gas a day.

An elephant has very small eyes in relation to its head. The eyes contain very few photoreceptors so vision is poor—they can't see more than a few hundred feet.

THE "EARPRINTS" OF AN ELEPHANT

The ears of an elephant are covered in veins that form a unique pattern for each animal. In fact, it is thought that elephants often recognize each other more by their ear patterns, than by sound or smell.

An elephant will cool itself by flapping its ears. The flapping of the blood-vessel-rich ears lowers the animal's body temperature by about 15 degrees Fahrenheit (–9.44 degrees Celsius).

Elephants have the biggest brains (about 12 pounds [5.44kg]) and the thickest skin (about 1 inch [2.5cm]) of any animal.

The elephant is the only animal with four knees.

An elephant's skin weighs from 992 to 1,654 pounds (450 to 750kg).

The tail of an adult elephant weighs about 24 pounds (11kg), about the same as its tongue.

Gorillas are the largest living primates, the family of animals that includes monkeys, apes, and humans.

Gorillas prefer the tropical forests that blanket parts of Central and West Africa. There are three subspecies of gorilla, each living in different parts of Africa. The *gorilla-gorilla* lives in the western lowlands; the *gorilla-graueri* lives in the eastern lowlands; and the *gorilla-berengei* lives in the mountains.

There are only about 35,000 gorillas presently in the wild. They live in Nigeria, Cameroon, Gabon, Congo, Rwanda, and Zaire.

There are about 600 gorillas living in captivity in zoos throughout the world.

An adult male gorilla can weigh from 300 to 500 pounds (136 to 227kg). A female weighs from 150 to 250 pounds (68 to 113kg).

The average arm span of an adult male gorilla is about nine feet (2.7m).

Gorillas recognize each other primarily by faces; after that, by body shape.

Every gorilla has a unique nose print.

A gorilla's favorite foods include bamboo, thistles, and wild celery. It also eats over 200 types of leaves, tubers, flowers, and fruits. Meat-eating is restricted to insects.

Gorillas do not drink water. They obtain all the moisture they need from the plants they consume—about 50 pounds (22.6kg) a day.

Although gorillas can't produce the same sounds as humans, they are capable of creating about 25 distinct hooting, screaming, and grunting noises.

A mature male gorilla is about as strong as six men.

Unlike humans, gorillas' arms are more massive and muscular than their legs.

A male gorilla becomes a "silverback" or family leader at about the age of 15 when the hair on his back turns a silvery gray.

A silverback gorilla has three or four adult females, who ordinarily stay with him for life.

Gorillas show a wide range of emotions, including vocalized crying and laughing. A delighted gorilla will jump in the air and grunt happily. A gorilla deprived of a companion will withdraw and show signs of depression.

A gorilla will build a new "sleeping nest" every night by bending flexible plants into a springy platform, usually on the ground or in low trees.

Gorillas sleep an average of 13 hours each night and several hours during the heat of the day.

Although they can't reproduce the sounds of human speech, gorillas are capable of understanding spoken languages and can learn to communicate in sign language.

Not as curious or excitable as its nearest relative, the chimpanzee, the gorilla nevertheless shows more persistence and memory retention in solving a problem and is more likely to perform a task out of interest than to earn a reward.

Gorillas may live about 35 years in the wild and up to 54 years in zoos.

Gorillas live in groups, or troops, from two to over 30 members.

Man is the gorilla's only enemy.

The word "giraffe" comes from the Arabic word *zirafah*, which means "the tallest of all."

The Egyptians and Greeks thought giraffes were a mixture of camel and leopard and had a special name for them that translates into "camel-leopard."

A giraffe has a modified joint in its neck that allows it to extend its head vertically, thus adding to its reach.

Female giraffes spend about ten hours a day grazing the crowns of trees. Males spend only about three hours a day grazing.

Giraffes have the same number of neck bones as humans: seven.

A giraffe will often clean its ears with its 24-inch (61cm) tongue.

The huge size of adult giraffes makes it unnecessary for them to travel in groups. They have few predators. However, baby giraffes are vulnerable to attack. One of their greatest enemies is the spotted hyena.

When baby giraffes are born, they drop six feet (1.8m) to the ground and land on their heads.

The tongue of a giraffe is bluish-black in color and is covered with a thick, sticky saliva that strips the foliage from trees with only a few licks.

THE "DEMOCRATIC" SOCIETY OF THE GIRAFFE

The giraffe is nonterritorial and sociable, living in loosely organized herds with no leaders. Herds may be composed of all males, all females, females and young, or both sexes. They may also contain giraffes of all ages.

A giraffe moves by walking slowly or by galloping. In each case, the entire weight of the animal is supported alternately by the right and left legs. The long neck acts as a counterbalance, extending away from the weight-supporting legs, and keeps the giraffe from toppling to one side.

To drink, a giraffe must straddle or bend its forelegs. This is when the animal is most vulnerable to attack, so giraffes restrict their drinking to safe places, often guarding one another.

Giraffes can go for over a month without water, probably because the straddling position they must take to drink makes them vulnerable. For the same reason, giraffes do not eat grass and low-lying bushes.

The top speed for a galloping giraffe is 37 miles (60km) per hour.

From 50 to 75 percent of giraffe calves fall prey to lions, cheetahs, and hyenas in their first months.

A mother giraffe will defend her calves against an attack by kicking. The huge force of a giraffe kick can shatter the ribcage of an adult lion.

THE MANY VOICES OF THE GIRAFFE

The idea that giraffes are mute is a myth. Although they are unusually quiet animals, calves bleat and make a mewing call, and mother giraffes (cows) seeking lost calves bellow. A male bull giraffe looking for a mate makes snorting or delicate flute-like sounds. Startled giraffes hiss or groan.

A male giraffe grows from 16 to 22 feet (5 to 7m) tall.

A fully grown male giraffe weighs about 2,000 pounds (907kg), or a ton.

Giraffes take their eight hours of sleep in "catnaps" throughout the day and evening. These can last from 10 minutes to two hours, during which time the giraffes may either lie down or remain standing. While napping, their eyes remain partly opened.

Every giraffe has unique markings. Giraffes recognize the individual members of a herd by these markings.

The brown blotches of a giraffe are an effective way of camouflaging the animal when it stands in or around the shadows of trees.

During the mating season, male giraffes fight for females by butting heads. But the contest is rarely violent and the "loser" always seems to know when he's bested by his opponent, bowing away gracefully.

Because their necks are so long, giraffes have vascular systems that are specially equipped with valves to prevent blood from draining out of their brains.

A giraffe has a life span of about 20 years.

A newborn giraffe calf is about 6 feet tall (1.8m) and weighs about 200 pounds (91kg). It can stand after only about 20 minutes after birth.

The hippopotamus is the third largest land animal. Only elephants and some species of rhinos are bigger.

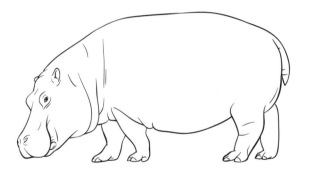

Hippos are mainly found along the Nile Valley and in game parks throughout Africa.

There are currently about 157,000 hippopotamuses in the wild—a quarter of the number of elephants.

Hippopotamuses travel in herds known as bloats.

A hippo can open its mouth wide enough to fit a four-foot-tall (122cm) child inside.

The lips of a hippopotamus are nearly two feet (61cm) wide.

A hippo grabs grass with its lips, and then swipes its head from side to side to tear off the stalks.

An adult male hippopotamus can weigh as much as 7,000 pounds (3,175kg). Females weigh about 4,000 pounds (1,800kg).

An angry adult hippopotamus can outrun a man.

A hippo's eyes, ears, and nostrils are all on the top of its head. This is so the hippo can almost completely submerge itself in water and yet still be aware of its surroundings.

THE AMAZING HIPPOPOTAMUS EYE

The hippo has one of the most unusual eyes in the animal kingdom. Its pupil is in the shape of an upside-down T, which allows it to split its vision above and below the water simultaneously while equalizing the light between the two halves of the image. The horizontal portion of the pupil is larger to compensate for less light underwater. The vertical portion of the pupil adjusts for light above water. Together, they make a balanced image that keeps the hippo visually aware of its environment.

The name *hippopotamus* comes from the Greek *hippos*, meaning "horse," and *potamus*, meaning "river." So the name means river-horse.

Hippos are the closest living land mammals to whales and dolphins.

Hippos give birth underwater. This keeps the calf from injuring itself by falling and instantly teaches it to swim.

Hippos can easily get sunburned on their half-inch thick skin. This is why they prefer muddy water.

HIPPOPOTAMUS SUNTAN LOTION

The hippopotamus has special glands in its skin that secret a reddish, oily liquid. It's believed this liquid protects the animal against the sun and may also be a kind of antibiotic for skin abrasions and injuries. The red liquid led to the folk belief that hippos could "sweat blood."

A hippopotamus has four toes placed very close together. They function almost as webbed feet and help the animal swim.

Because they sink in water, hippos prefer shallow lakes and streams where they can walk across the bottom. In deeper waters, they make short leaps, paddling between each one with their four-toed feet.

When a hippopotamus goes underwater, a reflex action causes its nose and ears to snap shut, making the animal watertight.

Hippopotamuses battle by using their heads as hammers. They also use their four teeth, which are very sharp.

A hippo with its mouth stretched open isn't yawning, it's threatening you.

A hippo can hold its breath for about five minutes.

Hippos use a very low frequency (infrasound) communication system that travels through many substances—water, air, solids—and over long distances. A similar system is used by elephants and whales.

Very affectionate, hippos can be seen nuzzling, playing, and resting their heads on one another.

The hippo's life span is about 35 years.

Well, maybe they're not all beautiful—and maybe some aren't that brainy, either. But all of these animals show ingenuity, resourcefulness, affection, and that mysteriously powerful trait called "instinct." Some have even learned sign language and invented new words! The details follow.

167

Chimpanzees are more closely related to humans than they are to gorillas. We share all but 1.4 percent of our DNA with chimps!

Chimpanzees live in a variety of habitats, as long as there are trees. These include rainforests, woodlands, and tree-studded grasslands.

Chimps once inhabited 25 African countries. Now they are found in fewer than 13 countries and in decreasing numbers.

Wild chimpanzees eat mostly fruit, seeds, leaves, and flowers, but are sometimes known to hunt and eat animals such as wild bush pigs and even small species of monkey.

Chimpanzee society consists of communities of 25 to 90 individuals.

A chimpanzee can be taught to recognize itself in a mirror. Other species of ape, including the gorilla, don't understand the image.

THOSE CHIMPS AND THEIR TOOLS!

Chimpanzees display high intelligence by using sticks, rocks, and leaves as tools. A young chimp instinctively knows how to crush a hard nut with a stone, or how to carefully insert a long stick into a termite colony to draw out the insects. Amazingly, chimps have even mastered cupping water in homemade baskets of leaves!

Zoologists believe that chimpanzees may eat certain plants for medicinal value. Tests have confirmed the presence of antibiotic and anti-parasitic properties in the plants chimps consume during the rainy season.

SIGNING CHIMPANZEES

In the mid 1970s, researchers began teaching chimps to communicate in American Sign Language. The remarkable results demonstrated that chimps had a huge capability for learning and communicating sophisticated thoughts and emotions. They also showed an inventive capacity never before known to humans. When the chimpanzee Washoe first saw a swan, she called it a "water bird." Another chimp, Moja, described a glass of Alka-Seltzer as "listen drink."

If chimps look at other chimps (or humans) and extend an arm or leg, they're asking to be groomed.

Chimp mothers enjoy lifelong bonds with their adult sons and daughters.

The rhesus monkey gives its name to the rhesus antigen, which was found in their blood in 1940. This discovery allowed scientists to identify the various blood groups in humans.

Rhesus monkeys roam freely through Afghanistan, India, Thailand, and Southern China. They have recently been introduced into the State of Florida to attract tourists.

Rhesus monkeys were the first primates to be sent into space.

Rhesus monkeys feed on seeds, roots, buds, fruit, insects, bark, and cereals. But their diet is so varied zoologists haven't yet fully identified it.

Rhesus monkeys coexist peacefully with human populations and are frequent visitors to domestic gardens in cities. However, they have been known to steal fruit from trees or even breakfast left on the table!

The zebra's closest relatives are horses and donkeys. Like them, the zebra has only one toe (with the nail formed into a hoof) on each foot.

Zebras live about 28 years in the wild and about 35 years in captivity.

A zebra can run up to 40 miles (65km) an hour.

It's believed that a zebra's stripes confuse predators by making it difficult for them to judge distances accurately. This means that a running zebra appears much farther away than it actually is.

A zebra's mane is striped in a pattern that exactly matches the pattern on its neck.

The zebra social group consists of a single male and a few females in a "harem." A dominant male zebra is constantly challenged by other males for possession of his harem.

The peak mating time for zebras is after a rainstorm.

Zebras are not currently an endangered species.

Zebras eat mostly grasses and spend most of their time grazing.

A lemur has one of the longest life spans of any primate—40 years.

Before eating a meal of millipedes, brown lemurs spit on them, crush them into a ball, and roll the ball between their hands. It's believed that the scent of the crushed millipedes has a pleasurable and intoxicating effect on the lemurs.

A lemur also enjoys the sap from trees that may have a spicy and sweet taste to it.

Lemurs are *cathemeral*, which means that they can be active at any time during a 24-hour period. However, when living in a group, they try to keep to the same waking and sleeping schedule.

Lemurs are arboreal, which means that they spend about 95 percent of their time in the upper branches of trees. They travel throughout forest canopies by crawling on all fours or leaping between branches.

The Diana monkey is named after the Greek goddess of hunting, Diana, because the white stripe across the monkey's head resembles the shape of a bow.

Diana monkeys have deep pouches in their cheeks that they use to carry food while they continue to forage.

Like the lemurs, Diana monkeys are arboreal and spend most of their lives in trees.

A typical group of Diana monkeys consists of 5 to 50 animals, with one dominant male and many females in a "harem."

In the wild, gazelles live about 15 years. In captivity, they live to be about 25.

The light body and long slender legs of the gazelle make it an excellent runner. Its large eyes and ears make it very sensitive to its surroundings.

Both male and female gazelles have ridged and curved horns. But the horns of the male are larger and are used for ritualized fighting during mating season.

A herd of gazelles can contain up to 200 animals. While migrating over long distances, herds break up into smaller groups with "scouts" looking ahead for water or food.

Gazelles have a sophisticated signaling system that allows an entire herd to detect danger and respond instantly. This is why a large herd of gazelles suddenly runs at the slightest hint of trouble.

BEWARE—WE CAN OUTRUN YOU. MAYBE.

One of the most important gazelle signals consists of "pronking" when a predator is detected. A gazelle will stiffen its legs, curve its back, and jump repeatedly in the air. Zoologists believe this behavior tells a predator that the herd is large, energetic, and can outrun the predator if chased—a kind of bluff. At the same time, the signaling gazelle warns other herd members that potential danger is close by.

Male gazelles have a special gland near the eye that secretes a scent used to mark out territories. This is why a gazelle will rub its face on a tree or bush.

Gazelles are plentiful and not currently endangered.

The chacma baboons of southern Africa can live without water for 120 days. They obtain all the liquid nourishment they need from fruits, leaves, and fleshy plants.

Baboons have one of the most varied social structures of all the apes. Groups, called "troops," may consist of all males, all females, or all females with one dominant male.

Baboons are not particularly good climbers and spend most of their time on the ground.

Male baboons will sometimes kill and eat infant baboons that are not related to them.

In 1986, a troop of baboons was found living in the heart of the Namib Desert, the most arid environment known to be inhabited by a nonhuman primate. The baboons ate figs for moisture.

Orangutan means "person of the forest." It combines the Malay words *orang* meaning "people," and *huntan,* meaning "forest."

Orangutans are the largest tree-living (arboreal) mammals. They avoid the high canopies of trees and prefer to live at the dense middle level where they are well-hidden and protected from the sun.

Orangutans have one of the longest life spans of the apes—about 60 years.

Orangutans are one of the most endangered species of apes. Only about 5,000 exist, in Indonesia and Borneo.

Deforestation of the orangutan habitat is responsible for the loss of about 1,000 orangutans each year.

Much valuable orangutan land has been converted to palm oil plantations since the oil sells for high prices on the world market.

An anteater belongs to a classification of animals called *monotremes*. These egg-laying mammals include the platypus.

The long and narrow shape of the African anteater's head evolved to house its long tongue.

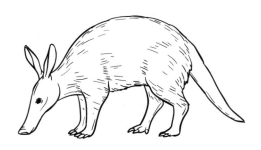

When feeding, the anteater sticks its tongue in and out over 100 times a minute to slurp up its food. It enjoys termites as well as ants.

When feasting on ants, anteaters are discriminating eaters. They recognize (by scent) the aggressive soldier ants and avoid eating them.

An anteater's tongue is covered with an adhesive glue that is about 100 times stickier than flypaper.

The long claws of the anteater evolved for digging, not for walking. In fact, walking is awkward for anteaters since they must curl up their claws and walk on their knuckles.

An anteater rests for up to 15 hours a day, sleeping in a scooped-out hollow and covering itself with its tail.

Anteaters have poor vision and get around mostly by using their senses of smell and hearing. In fact, they often detect a termite nest by hearing the insects within their mounds.

Anteaters have one of the lowest metabolic rates of any warm-blooded animal. This allows them to move slowly, conserve energy, and go for long periods without eating.

The koala "bear" is Australia's national emblem.

The koala isn't really a bear, but a marsupial (like the kangaroo) and belongs to a species all its own.

On a koala's front paws, the first and second digits oppose the other three—almost like twin thumbs. This arrangement allows the koala to grip branches as it climbs trees.

The koala prefers to eat eucalyptus leaves, but it also enjoys foliage from acacias. It eats about 17.6 ounces (500g) of fresh leaves daily.

ODD APPETITE OF THE KOALA

Even though the koala prefers the eucalyptus tree, its foliage is low in nutrients, high in indigestible wood fiber (lignin), and laced with toxins. But koalas are able to detoxify the poisons in their liver and excrete them. They also have the longest intestines of all mammals, to help them digest difficult foods.

The strong eucalyptus oil, absorbed into the bloodstream of the koala, seems to act as a bug repellent, keeping the animal free from parasites. It also makes the koala smell like a cough drop!

Koalas obtain all the water they need from eating foliage. In fact, "koala" is an aboriginal word meaning "no drink."

Koalas have a very small brain—less than 2 percent of their body weight. This probably evolved as an adaptation to their low-energy diet.

Koalas have a very low metabolism and spend up to 80 percent of their time sleeping. Less than 10 percent is spent feeding and the rest of their waking time is spent just moving around. Although they are good climbers, they are very slow walkers.

Koalas are very solitary animals and are most active during the night.

Koalas don't have sweat glands. They lower their body temperature by licking their arms.

Patas monkey troops consist mostly of females, with a dominant female leader and only one or two passive males.

Zoologists have identified the patas monkey as the fastest primate. It runs on all fours and can reach speeds of up to 34 miles (55km) per hour.

The spider monkey gets its name from its extremely long tail and long spidery limbs. In fact, seen from a distance, a spider monkey's tail is practically indistinguishable from its limbs, making it look like a five-legged creature.

The tail of the spider monkey is as useful as its limbs. The monkey uses the tail to grasp branches and swing from them.

Although they are quadrupeds, spider monkeys can also walk on two legs across the tree canopy—that is, when they're not swinging!

The proboscis monkeys have the longest noses of all primates—almost a quarter of their body length!

Zoologists believe the long noses of proboscis monkeys function as both a visual and aural signal used during mating season.

When looking for a mate, male proboscis monkeys vocalize through their noses, making honking and squeaking sounds. They also shake their noses to attract a female's attention.

Proboscis monkeys live exclusively on the island of Borneo, south of the continent of Australia.

A newborn kangaroo is about the size of a peanut and is called a joey.

After a 38-day gestation period, a joey climbs up through its mother's fur into her pouch, and looks for milk. It will say there for nearly 300 days!

Even after leaving its mother's pouch, a joey will continue to feed on mother's milk until it's 18 months old.

A group of kangaroos is called a mob. Despite the name, mobs usually consist of only four to eight kangaroos, equally divided between males and females.

A full-grown kangaroo can leap up to 30 feet (9m) in a single bound.

Besides leaping, an adult kangaroo can run—on two legs—at speeds of up to 30 miles (48km) per hour. When moving slowly, they crawl around on all fours.

Their amazing leaping ability is also the cause for kangaroo-killing among sheep farmers, who shoot the animals to prevent them from leaping fences and feeding on valuable grazing land.

The unique metabolism of a kangaroo allows it to use less energy the faster it runs.

The kangaroo population is distributed throughout Australia, including the island of Tasmania. About two million of them exist, and they are not currently endangered.

Kangaroos are least active during the day. They rest in the shade or in shallow holes they've dug in the earth.

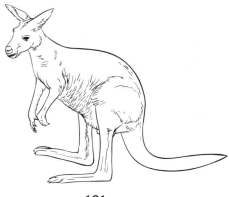

The impala, a grazing African antelope, lives in single-sex herds.

Impalas need a daily supply of water and will mark out their territories within a few hours of discovering a freshwater supply. Unfortunately, because of this, impala predators know where to look for them.

Impalas have hair-trigger reflexes and seem to know, almost before the fact, when danger is approaching.

The lyre-shaped horns of the male impala are among the most beautiful of all the horned animals of the family *Bovidae*, which includes bison, goats, and sheep.

After a baby impala is born, its mother conceals it for a few weeks, visiting only occasionally to nurse it.

When a baby impala is weaned and strong enough to get around on its own, it joins a band of other young impalas. Much of its time is spent "playing" with this group—which is thought to encourage the development of strong running muscles.

When the African meerkat emerges from its underground burrow in the morning, adults will stand erect on two legs, watching for predators, before venturing out. Despite its name, the meerkat is actually a type of mongoose—a small, bushy-tailed meat-eater that feeds on rodents.

The meerkat doesn't design its own habitat, but often takes over the burrows of ground squirrels. It enlarges these burrows by digging with its sharp claws.

A group of meerkats is called a colony. It can contain as many as 30 animals.

Adult meerkats take turns watching for predators. If a predator—like an eagle—is sighted, the sentries give warning barks and the colony flees underground.

Upon sighting a snake, adult meerkats will huddle together and advance in a group towards the snake. This usually drives the snake away.

After their "shift" is over and no danger is present, the male meerkat sentries will snooze in the sun or forage for small insect snacks. The females will usually tend to their young.

The naked mole rat, living in East Africa, gets its name from its almost hairless pink skin.

The mole rat lives in underground colonies of about 80 animals. Only one female in the colony breeds, and her offspring become workers—helping to dig the burrows in search of edible tubers.

The most prominent feature of the mole rat is its huge, shovel-shaped front teeth, used—obviously!—for digging.

The eyes of the mole rat are tiny and can only detect light and dark.

The body of the mole rat is round and cylindrical and its limbs are short and powerful. Its ears are tiny and close to the surface of its skin. This design streamlines it for underground movement.

The skin of the mole rat is extremely flabby, which allows the rat to push dirt around itself as it burrows.

Although most mole rat offspring become workers, some grow larger than others and become mole rat "soldiers." Should the mother (breeding) mole rat die, then a female soldier will become a breeder to replace her.

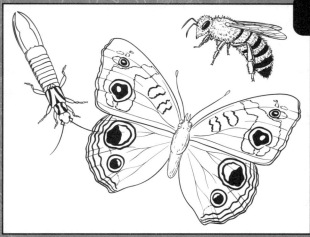

7

Scientists will probably never know just how many different types of insect exist. There are just too many! A million years after human beings have vanished from Earth, insect societies will flourish. Right now, there's probably just such a society right under that stone in your garden. Read more about the creepy-crawlies and get the heebie-jeebies.

The word insect comes from the Latin *insecare*, which means "divided into parts."

There are more than a million different types of insects, with new types discovered every few months. This means that 75 percent of all animal species described by scientists are insects.

Insect pests eat one-third of the world's food crop each year.

All insects are arthropods, a type of animal that lacks a backbone. In addition to insects, arthropods include jellyfish, corals, amoebas, and crustaceans.

Insects are unique among the arthropods because they have exoskeletons. This means that their bodies are supported by a hard external shell rather than internal bones.

Insect mouth parts have evolved specifically for biting and sucking plant tissues.

Insects breathe through holes along their abdomens called spiracles.

Insects have specialized organs called *malpighian tubules*, which act as kidneys. The tubules clean an insect's blood of waste products and deposit the waste into the abdomen for eventual excretion.

All insects have two antennae. Besides providing the sense of smell, antennae also help the insect balance itself while flying.

An insect's compound eyes are made from thousands of hexagonal lenses. This allows an insect to see in practically all directions at once.

The biggest insect in the world lived about 250 million years ago. It was a primitive dragonfly called the *meganeura,* and it had a wingspan of about two feet (61cm)!

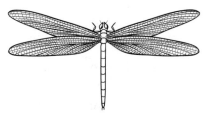

Collembola, the insects known as springtails, have also been around for a very long time. This is one of the oldest insect orders with fossil remains known from the Devonian period, 408 to 360 million years ago.

Monarch butterflies can fly an average of 30 miles (48km) per day and usually migrate long distances at low altitudes. However, Monarchs can endure high altitudes and will sometimes fly as high as a mile above land.

WINGS—THE KEY TO AN INSECT'S SUCCESS

Most insects have wings—a key to their success and survival. Wings allow insects to disperse widely and escape unfavorable environmental changes. Flight also allows them to escape predators and to colonize new environments where food is plentiful. Insects lay thousands of eggs and evolve rapidly.

Insects evolved during the Devonian Period—408 to 360 million years ago—long before the first dinosaurs.

A type of insect and flower "color coordination" exists in nature. The bright color of a flower means, inevitably, that some type of insect can see it and be attracted to that color.

Depending on what plant parts they eat, insects can be classified as leaf eaters, sap feeders, wood and bark feeders, and seed eaters.

The science of studying ants is called myrmecology.

Ants, bees, and termites are the most "sociable" insects. They live together in huge colonies, ruled by a queen and protected by "soldiers."

Worker ants are usually female. Besides finding food, they clean the colony and tend to the queen's eggs. Soldiers are a specialized type of male worker ant. They have powerful jaws to defend the queen and colony from invaders.

Besides biting, some species of ant—such as the wood ant—defend themselves and their colony by spraying formic acid on intruders.

Many species of ants feed on the sugary secretions produced by another insect—the aphid.

A wandering ant will leave a chemical scent behind called a *pheromone*. Secreted from the abdomen, pheromone signals help ants follow each other and convey basic information, such as the direction of a food source.

Huge swarms of ants flying in summer signal mating time. Male ants attract queens as they fly, and mating takes place in midair. After a queen mates in midair, she no longer needs her wings and sheds them.

Like most insects, ants have two compound eyes. These are made up of many hexagonal lenses that focus light from each part of the insect's field of vision onto the rhabdome, the equivalent of a human retina.

The average caterpillar has 16 legs and 248 muscles in its head.

The jaws of the caterpillar are called *mandibles*. They evolved to bite off plant material and chew it into small, easily digestible pieces.

Maxillae are the caterpillar's mouthparts that taste plant material and determine whether or not it's suitable for consumption. During metamorphosis, these evolve into the butterfly's long sucking tube, called the proboscis.

Caterpillars have a very limited diet, some preferring the leaves of only one type of plant.

Caterpillars may have venom sacs under their spines. Touching their spines can cause severe irritation to sensitive humans.

Some types of caterpillars feed on poisonous plants.

The "great fleshy horn" of the common tomato cater-pillar evolved to scare away predators—and curious humans!

The original name for the butterfly was "flutterby."

All butterflies have four wings.

Butterfly wings are covered with delicate, overlapping scales. The mosaic pattern of these scales, which often refract light, give butterflies their unique wing patterns.

Butterflies can detect whether or not a plant is good for them the moment they land on it. This is because they taste with their feet!

One of a butterfly's favorite flowers is the buddleia, also known as the "butterfly bush."

Although both butterflies and moths have four wings, the wings of the moth are usually colorless and drab compared with the wings of the butterfly.

When butterflies rest, they fold their wings together. Moths rest with their wings open.

Butterflies rest at night and are active during the day. Moths sleep all day and fly all night.

Butterflies have long, slender antennae. Moths have shorter, feather-shaped antennae.

The adult Morgan's Sphinx moth from Madagascar has a tube mouth, or proboscis, from 12 to 14 inches (30 to 36cm) long. It enables the moth to reach nectar deep within large orchids. Between meals, it coils up like a garden hose.

The eye spots on some species of butterfly wings are there to fool predators into thinking that the insect is in fact a much larger and fiercer creature.

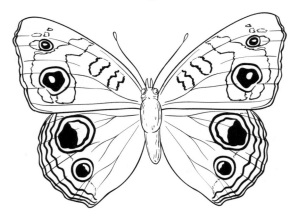

The butterfly's average flight speed is 6 miles (9km) per hour. The hawk moth can fly 11 miles (18km) per hour. But neither can compare with the tabanid fly (related to the horse fly) whose speed has been clocked at 90 miles (145km) per hour.

INSECT MIMICRY

Entomologists (the scientists who study insects) have noticed that a group of unrelated species of insects can have similar markings. This is called "Batesian mimicry." Many vulnerable insects evolve the markings of more poisonous species to fool a predator into leaving them alone. For example, the Viceroy butterfly mimics the wing pattern of the poisonous Monarch. Another type of mimicry, called "Müllerian mimicry," occurs when two poisonous species have similar markings. Acting as a kind of "poison flag," this type of mimicry ensures that fewer poisonous insects have to be sacrificed in order to teach the predators to leave them alone.

The male gypsy moth can "smell" the virgin female gypsy moth from 1.8 miles (2.9km) away.

The word "beetle" comes from the word *bitula* in Old English, meaning "to bite."

There are currently 300,000 known species of beetle. They are the most successful group of insects in the world and are found on land in every continent except Antarctica.

Most beetles have wings, but not all species can fly.

Beetles have a pair of armored wing-covers, called elytra. The true flying wings lie beneath the elytra.

The hard covering of beetles is made from chitin, a substance similar to human fingernails.

The nocturnal dung beetle's eyes allow it to see the direction of moonbeams in order to navigate.

Dung beetles are also known as tumblebugs.

Beetles have a very varied diet and will eat just about anything. Some, like the dung beetle, enjoy dung and roll it into balls using their rear legs.

The woodworm, a notorious destroyer of furniture, is actually a beetle. It eats wood, boring small holes through it as it travels.

The African Goliath beetle is the heaviest insect in the world. It can grow up to 6.3 inches (16cm) long and can weigh over 3.5 ounces (100g).

The stag beetle gets its name from its huge lower jaws that look like the antlers of a stag. During the mating season, the males use their jaws to fight male rivals.

The ladybug belongs to the beetle family. Its bright red shell warns predators that it tastes nasty.

Although most beetle species are considered pests, the ladybug is beneficial to agriculture because it eats aphids and mealybugs. A ladybug can eat as many as 5,000 aphids in its year-long life.

The number of spots identifies the age of ladybugs. As ladybugs age, their spots fade.

The pyralis firefly, or "lightning bug," is a common beetle in North America.

Fireflies use their flash to attract other fireflies. Males flash about every five seconds while females flash every two seconds.

The brightness of a single firefly is one-fortieth that of a candle.

The luminescence of the firefly is caused by the chemical luciferin. The firefly can control its luciferin to regulate its flash.

Fireflies are carnivores and will even eat each other!

Male earwigs have large, rounded pincers. Females have straighter ones.

Earwigs use their pincers to eat, to defend themselves, and in courtship displays.

Earwigs are nocturnal and can completely strip a large tomato plant of its leaves in a single night.

Earwigs have nothing to do with people's ears. They are a type of common beetle that feeds on sweet plants and on other insects.

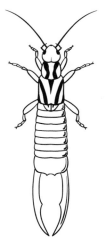

A newborn earwig, called a nymph, is completely transparent. Within a week its body will darken and take on the familiar brownish-red earwig color.

A DEVOTED MOTHER EARWIG

Female earwigs are some of the best "parents" in the insect world. After she lays a cluster of eggs, the mother earwig will guard them until they hatch. If the eggs get disturbed by slight movements in the soil, the mother earwig will carefully pick each one up in her mouth and put them all back in a neat little pile. She'll also clean her eggs, removing dirt and fungi, by gently turning them over in her mouth.

Cockroaches can survive underwater for up to 15 minutes.

Termites found in Australia can build mounds 20 feet (6m) high and at least 100 feet (30m) wide.

Globally, termites outweigh human beings 10 to 1.

Like ants and termites, common wasps live in colonies with one queen. The location of a nest depends on where the queen lands. The other wasps follow in a swarm, settle, and build a nest around her.

There are many types of wasp, but the familiar "yellow jacket" has a striped yellow and black body. It's attracted to sugary foods and drink, and is a common unwelcome visitor at picnics.

Wasps are extremely protective of their nests, which they build in the spring. The nests can be attached to practically anything—a house, roof, tree trunk, or lamppost—as long as the location is warm and dry.

By the end of the summer, a wasp nest can be the size of a football and contain many thousands of cells.

Wasps build their nests by chewing small pieces of wood into a paste. The paste hardens into a rough paper "balloon" with many hexagonal compartments. The queen lays one egg in each compartment.

As the weather gets colder the wasps begin to die, leaving only a newly hatched queen to hibernate over the winter months. In the spring, the queen will fly with her new swarm and find a location for a new nest.

There are over 2,800 species of stick insects worldwide. They are found mostly in tropical and subtropical regions.

Stick insects are the longest insects in the world. The largest species come from Borneo and can reach 12 inches (30cm).

Stick insects are usually green or brown. Many have small bumps along their bodies so that they further resemble twigs!

Although stick insects are successful at disguising themselves, they must also stay very still to avoid their worst predators—birds.

Most stick insects are female. The female can lay fertile eggs without mating.

The eggs of a stick insect can lay dormant for up to three years before hatching.

Like stick insects, aphids lay fertile eggs without ever having mated. Only 10 days after hatching, aphid babies can give birth themselves.

After eating, a housefly regurgitates its food and then eats it again!

The flea can jump 350 times its body length. That is like a human jumping the length of about seven football fields.

The katydid bug hears through holes in its hind legs.

Dragonflies can travel 50 miles (80.5km) per hour and are one of the fastest flying insects in the world.

A dragonfly's first six months of life are spent underwater. After this time, it comes out of the water, sheds its outer skin, and starts flying. But if it falls in the water after it has shed its skin, it drowns.

A dragonfly feeds by catching insects in midair with its long legs.

The compound eye of the dragonfly is one of the most complex in the animal kingdom—with over 30,000 lenses.

The dragonfly has a long life cycle—about three years from egg to adult. But the adult stage of a dragonfly's life lasts only a few weeks.

Dragonfly nymphs hatch underwater and have gills for breathing.

A dragonfly nymph can spend as much as two years underwater. After that time, the nymph crawls out of the water, sheds its skin, and a winged dragonfly emerges.

After hatching from underwater eggs, dragonfly nymphs feed on tadpoles and small fish.

Mosquitoes have "teeth"—actually a saw-like part of their mouth that they use to drill into flesh.

Only the female mosquito "bites"; the male does not.

Mosquitoes flap their wings nearly 500 times per second.

A cricket must be full-grown before it can chirp. Only then are its wings large and thick enough to produce a chirping sound when rubbed together.

There have been more crickets launched into space than humans.

The frequency of cricket chirps is related to air temperature, with warmer temperatures resulting in more chirps per minute. To calculate the temperature (Fahrenheit) from the frequency of cricket chirps, count the number of chirps in 15 seconds and add 40.

Grasshoppers are closely related to crickets. You can tell them apart because crickets have long, thin antennae while grasshoppers' feelers are much shorter.

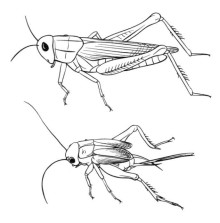

Male grasshoppers "sing," or stridulate, by rubbing their back legs against their wings. This is done to attract females.

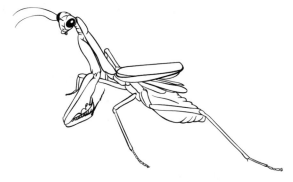

Grasshoppers can leap 20 times their own body length.

The praying mantis (*Stagmomantis carolina*) gets its name from the peculiar design of its jointed and serrated forelegs, which bend into a "praying" position. Its powerful legs hold the prey while the mantis consumes it.

The praying mantis is the only insect that can twist its head from side to side.

PRAYING MANTIS BAT DETECTOR

Entomologists recently discovered the function of the hollow resonating chamber within the abdomen of the mantis. The chamber evolved to help the mantis detect one of its most fearsome predators—the bat. When a mantis "hears" the echolocation squeaks of a bat, it knows it had better dive away and seek shelter.

After mating, the female praying mantis rips the male's head off.

The egg case of a praying mantis is called an *ootheca* and may contain 30–500 eggs.

Because it consumes such a wide variety of common pests, including the mosquito, the praying mantis is a protected species in many parts of the world.

A leech can drink up to eight time its weight in blood at one sitting.

If you weighed all the earthworms in the United States, they'd be about 55 times heavier than the combined weight of all the people in the country.

Earthworms have five hearts.

Some ribbon worms will eat themselves if they can't find any food.

There are over 30,000 species of bee worldwide, but commercial farmers rely on only about 11 species to pollinate their crops.

In the United States alone, about $14 billion worth of crops rely on pollination by a single type of bee—the European (common) honeybee.

The honeybee is a social insect and lives within the complex social structure of the hive, which it will defend ferociously against intruders. Honeybees do not need to hibernate. They use the same hive from one year to the next.

Most bees are covered with fine bristly hair. Honeybees even have a type of hair on their eyes!

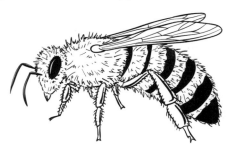

Bees see ultraviolet light, which allows them to navigate—even on cloudy days.

The honeybee flaps its wings about 300 times a second.

Honeybees require two different types of food. One is honey—made from nectar extracted from flowers—and the other is pollen. Honey provides the bee with energy, and pollen supplies the protein. All the vitamins a bee needs are contained in honey and pollen.

Most bee stings cause only localized pain and swelling. But if a person is highly allergic to bee venom, a dangerous reaction called anaphylaxis can occur. This condition causes such intense swelling that the victim is in danger of suffocating.

THE STICKY STING OF A HONEYBEE

The stinging organ of a honeybee is barbed so that it can't easily be removed from the skin. When a person is stung, the stinger (with its venom gland still attached) will tear away from the bee's body, killing the bee. But the venom gland continues to pump venom through the detached stinger! For this reason, never squeeze the site of a bee sting because it forces more venom into the wound. Instead, scrape it out of the skin using your fingernail.

POLLINATION EXPLAINED

As a bee climbs over flowers gathering nectar, its body is dusted with pollen. As it moves from flower to flower, the pollen passes from the male parts of the flower to the female parts, and pollinates them. This ensures the production of new seeds and regenerates the plant.

Honey is primarily of vegetable origin. Its sugars are formed by a mixture of sun, water, carbon dioxide, and special chemicals produced in the body of the bee.

THE AMAZING BEE DANCE

When it finds a rich source of nectar or pollen, a worker bee returns to the hive and communicates its discovery to other bees in a "bee dance." The dance is actually a series of movements that conveys specific information. If the bee vibrates its wings while walking in a circle, it means that the food is within 328 feet (100m) of the hive. If the food is farther away, the dance will take the form of a figure eight. The direction in which the bee moves and at what speed tells the others exactly where the food is located.

Honeybees sometimes mix pollen with honey to make "bee bread," a nutritious snack.

To make beeswax, the youngest bees clump together to raise their body temperature. Wax-producing glands under their abdomens excrete scales of wax about the size of a pinhead. Other worker bees "harvest" the wax scales and take them to the part of the hive that needs the wax.

Bees require the energy from about six pounds (2.72kg) of honey to produce about one pound (0.45kg) of wax.

The single queen is the largest bee of the hive. She leaves the hive only to mate—which she does while flying—and then returns to the hive to lay her eggs.

Only one of a queen bee's eggs will survive to become the new queen. The first bee to hatch and emerge from its cell will break open the cells of the competing bees and bite them to death.

THE CURIOUS CHEMISTRY OF HONEY-MAKING

Honeybee workers collect nectar each day to take back to the hive. The nectar is sucked from the flower and stored in a special stomach. When the bee returns to the hive, it regurgitates its nectar to another bee that adds enzymes from special glands. This mixture, deposited in the comb and sealed with a beeswax cap, ripens into honey as its moisture content drops from about 70 percent to 15 percent.

Beeswax, the substance bees secrete to build their combs, is a base for many cosmetic products. It's also used to make furniture polish and candles.

Beeswax is useful commercially because it doesn't easily melt and can remain solid to about 140 degrees Fahrenheit (60 degrees Celsius).

BIRTH OF THE KILLER BEES

Africanized bees, also called "killer bees," descended from Southern African bees that were imported into Brazil in 1956. At the time, Brazilian scientists were trying to breed a honey-producing bee better suited to the tropics. When some of the African bees escaped quarantine and began breeding with local Brazilian honeybees, a new type of aggressive bee was born, which multiplied quickly and began spreading throughout South and Central America.

Although their venom is no worse than ordinary honey bees, killer bees gets their reputation from their extreme aggressiveness. They will swarm and attack people and animals who unknowingly stray into their territory, even if the hive is not threatened.

The killer bee, like the honey bee, dies when it stings.

Once disturbed, a colony of killer bees remains agitated for up to 24 hours and will continue to attack people and animals within a range of a half-mile (0.81 km) of the hive.

Killer bees have proliferated widely because they're less discriminating in their choice of hive locations than are ordinary honeybees.

Scientists have recognized, so far, a single benefit that killer bees provide to the environment. When the bees pollinate coffee plants, the plants increase their yield by more than 50 percent.

Because of its eight legs, a spider is not classified as an insect but an arachnid, a group that includes scorpions, mites, and ticks.

There are about 20,000 species of spider.

Spiders have two body segments to an insect's three. The spider's abdomen houses its heart, reproductive organs, and silk glands. The front portion of the spider, called the *prosoma*, contains its brains, jaws, eyes, and stomach.

Spiders produce three distinct web designs—the cobweb, the orb web, and the triangle web.

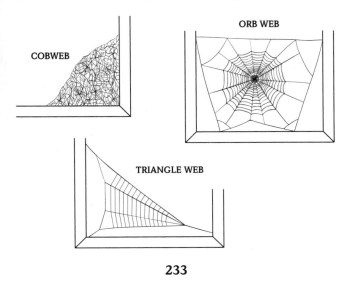

COBWEB

ORB WEB

TRIANGLE WEB

The bite of a poisonous spider rarely kills a healthy adult human.

You are more likely to be killed by a Champagne cork than by a poisonous spider.

The bite of the brown recluse spider can lead to widespread tissue damage called necrosis. It is one of the most dangerous spiders found in North America.

The venom of a female black widow spider is 15 times as poisonous as that of the prairie rattlesnake.

How did the black widow spider get its name? The female usually eats the smaller male after mating.

Besides feasting on insects such as flies, moths, and crickets, black widows enjoy small reptiles, snails, and slugs.

Once the prey is caught in its web, a black widow kills it by injecting venom through hollow fangs. The venom "pre-digests" the victim's flesh, allowing the spider to eventually suck it out.

Female black widows are about 1½ inches (3.8cm) across and have a characteristic red hourglass mark on their undersides. Males are smaller, have longer legs, and red and yellow markings.

Both male and female black widow spiders are poisonous, but the venom of the female is about 100 times stronger than that of the male.

The web of a black widow is tangled and basket-like and usually close to the ground. This allows the web to capture both flying and crawling insects.

The tips of the black widow's legs are covered with a slick oil that keeps the spider from sticking to its own web.

Baby spiders are called "spiderlings." They look exactly like the adult spider except for their tiny size and light color.

Newly hatched spiderlings aren't poisonous but they are cannibals and will eat each other if hungry.

All spiders are meat-eaters (carnivores). Although most eat insects, the larger spiders like tarantulas will eat many other small animals.

Most spiders live only about a year. The tarantula can live for up to 15 years.

Spiders produce the silk for their webs in special abdominal glands called spinnerets.

SPIDER AQUALUNG

Although spiders' silk is used mostly for building webs, spiders will also use their silk for shelter, cocoons, as a way of moving from place to place, and for diving bells—a special air-trapping sac some species of spider use to capture prey underwater.

Ounce for ounce, spiders' silk is stronger than steel.

In some species of spider, the mother dies when the young mature. The newly independent spiderlings eat her carcass before building their own webs.

Stretched into a single thread, a pound of spider webs will go around the earth two times.

There are about 10,000 species of mites and ticks.

There are about 600 species of scorpions.

Scorpions are commonly thought of as desert animals, but in fact, they occur in many other habitats as well, including grasslands, forests, and caves. They have even been found under snow-covered rocks at elevations high in the Andes Mountains of South America and the Himalayas of Asia.

8

The bear came over the mountain. So did the moose, porcupine, skunk, and hedgehog—all beautiful creatures that roam about in the wild places of the world. Learn about the animals that thrive in canyons, woods, rivers, grasslands, and snowy tundras.

239

A hedgehog's heart beats about 300 times a minute. But during hibernation, it slows to about 20 beats per minute, and the hedgehog's body temperature drops to 50 degrees Fahrenheit (10 degrees Celsius).

Most old or sick hedgehogs die during their hibernation period, from late fall to the following spring.

When threatened, a hedgehog can roll up into a tight ball, protected by its spines.

Badgers communicate best by smelling each other. Each badger has a completely unique smell and is recognized by that smell.

The honey badger can withstand hundreds of African bee stings without apparent harm.

A female ferret can die if she goes into heat and can't find a mate.

A beaver can swim underwater for up to 15 minutes.

A beaver has webbed feet and can swim about 5 miles (8km) per hour.

THE BEAVER ENGINEERS

Beavers build dome-shaped lodges from sticks and mud. The lodge has only underwater entrances. If the local pond or river water isn't deep enough, beavers will build a dam downstream from where they want their lodge. The dam ensures that there will be water around the lodge deep enough so that it doesn't freeze solid during the winter and block the entrance.

Beavers mate for life.

Beaver babies are called kits.

Beavers don't hibernate in winter, but stay mainly in their lodge where they've stockpiled enough food to last until spring.

Up to three generations of beavers often live together in one lodge, where they're protected from wolves and bears.

The beaver has a two-layer coat that's virtually waterproof. Underneath the shiny guard hairs, a silky underfur keeps the beaver's skin dry and warm.

Beavers use their sharp front teeth to cut down over 200 trees each year. They can cut through a foot-wide (30cm) tree overnight!

There are about 25 species of rabbit. A species of rabbit is found on every continent except Antarctica.

Although closely related, hares differ from rabbits in that they're born with fur and opened eyes, and can hop almost immediately. They're also larger, have stronger hind legs, and can leap much farther than rabbits.

HARE

RABBIT

Jackrabbits differ from other rabbits in their huge, long ears. The name comes from the fact that their ears resemble those of jackasses (donkeys).

When a rabbit licks its ears, it's doing more than just cleaning them. The rabbit ingests the oil on its ears because it contains a chemical that breaks down sunlight to produce vitamin D.

A female hare is a doe, a male is a buck, and the baby is a leveret.

There are about 30 species of mole worldwide living in habitats as varied as deserts and swamps.

A healthy mole can tunnel through 300 feet (90m) of earth in one day. After tiring themselves out with all that digging, moles create special resting rooms lined with dry grass.

A molehill is just the mound of earth the mole leaves behind as it excavates an underground tunnel.

Moles' best-developed sense is touch. They have special bumps on their snouts to amplify touch, and special sensory hairs on their feet and tails.

A MOLE'S EARTHWORM PANTRY

A mole's favorite meal is earthworms, which it stores alive in its tunnels. To keep the earthworms from escaping, the mole disables them by biting off their heads! It's not unusual for an adult mole to have 300 wiggling worms stored in a cool chamber.

The moose is the largest member of the deer family and is found in the forests of North America, Europe, and Asia.

Although the North American moose and European elk belong to the same species (*alces alces*), the elk is the smaller and more sociable animal. During the summer months, it lives in herds of up to 400 animals.

Moose have a strong musky scent that is used both for identification and for attracting a mate.

Moose have one of the loudest calls of all mammals and are fast runners.

The male moose is called a bull and has antlers. The antlers shed each year and grow back. The female is called a mare and has no antlers.

The main predator of the moose is the grizzly bear.

Although a type of weasel, the wolverine looks like a miniature bear and has a bear-sized appetite.

Wolverines were overhunted for their coats and are now protected by law in many countries. In 1900 they were practically extinct, but their numbers have increased considerably since then.

Wolverines eat almost anything, including the meat of dead animals.

A wolverine's jaws are among the most powerful in the animal kingdom. An adult wolverine can crush the bones of animals as large as caribou and moose.

Wolverines sometimes kill more than they can eat, so they bury the surplus underground.

The porcupine spends most of its time in trees looking for food.

A porcupine's top front teeth continue to grow throughout its life. When the teeth get too long, the porcupine gnaws on hard woods, even rocks, to wear them down.

A calm porcupine keeps its quills flat against its body. An excited porcupine contracts its skin so that the quills stand straight out—the better to stick a predator that comes too close.

Porcupines float in water! This is because their quills are hollow.

Reindeer are the only deer in which both sexes have antlers.

Reindeer and humans have been acquainted for about 8,000 years. Their relationship forms the basis for hunting and herding cultures throughout the Arctic.

Reindeer were once found in all northern latitudes, but because of extensive hunting, they've been reduced to isolated herds in Canada, Russia, and Scandinavia.

Reindeer feed on lichen that they find buried in snow. Lichen is also called "reindeer moss."

The flat, cleft hooves of the reindeer are adapted for walking on snow, and in the summer for walking on spongy arctic tundra.

THE TELLTALE CLICK OF THE REINDEER WALK

Reindeer make a clicking sound as they walk due to tendons snapping across a bone in the foot. This sound can be heard for nearly a hundred feet and, unfortunately, helps hunters know when a reindeer is near.

The two-layered coat of a reindeer is designed to trap air to insulate the animal against cold. The coat also allows the reindeer to lie on the snow without melting it or getting wet.

Reindeer lose about a quarter of their body weight during the winter months.

Reindeer are good swimmers. Their dense coats hold air and keep them buoyant in water, and their broad feet act like paddles.

A female reindeer will give birth to only one calf in the spring. A calf can run an hour after its birth.

Reindeer are found in some of the largest herds and are among the most widely migrating mammals. Herds 10,000 strong can travel up to 4,971 miles (8,000km) in the spring and winter.

The white-tailed deer is one of the shyest of mammals. It will sprint away at the slightest sound or motion.

A healthy deer has a life span of about 12 years.

Bucks (male deer) can weigh up to 400 pounds (180kg). Does (female deer) weigh about half that.

Only bucks have antlers, which they shed every year.

Baby deer are called fawns. They're usually born in May or June.

One of a deer's favorite foods is acorns.

The bold black and white coat of a skunk warns predators that it has a secret weapon.

Skunks are scavengers and will eat almost anything—even dead fish!

Spotted skunks will do practically anything to scare a predator without using their spray—even handstands! Other species of skunk will wave their bushy tails.

Skunk spray is also an irritant and can temporarily blind a predator if it gets into the eyes.

READY, AIM, FIRE!

A skunk's spray is created in two glands just behind the tail and fired from nozzles in the skunk's anal glands. The jets of oily, yellow liquid can travel up to 10 feet (3m). The skunk can even twist its nozzles to aim its spray in any direction. The spray itself has chemical properties that cause it to cling to substances and evaporate very slowly. This means that skunk stench can last a very long time!

WHAT DO PRONGHORNS AND SKUNKS HAVE IN COMMON?

An alarmed pronghorn antelope makes its hair stand up on end to reveal more of its white rump. Also, like a skunk, the pronghorn has scent glands near the tail that eject a strong-smelling spray.

The pronghorn antelopes are the fastest mammals in North America, running up to 60 miles (97km) per hour.

Female pronghorns give birth to twins more than 50 percent of the time.

Pronghorns are the only living animals with double-branched horns that they keep for life.

THE DANGEROUS INDIGESTION OF COWS

Recently, scientists have determined that gas produced from 1.3 billion belching cows the world over adds dangerous levels of methane to the atmosphere. Along with carbon dioxide, methane is one of the key gases responsible for the "greenhouse effect." Cows, along with sheep, goats, camels, and buffalo, are ruminants. These animals regurgitate food in a cud, chew it, and then re-swallow it for further digestion. Cows have four stomachs, and each regurgitation between stomachs is accompanied by a methane belch. To meet the belching crisis, scientists are investigating ways of adding organic substances to the diets of cows that will allow them to digest without the gassy aftereffect. To do this, they're studying the stomach chemistry of another, quieter class of ruminant—the kangaroo!

The black bear is found mostly in North American forests. Although gentle and curious by nature, it can be dangerous when with its young or when searching for food.

The black bear is a quadruped, but will rear up on its hind legs to scare an enemy.

Black bears have poor eyesight but an excellent sense of smell.

Like all bears, the black bear is flat-footed (plantigrade). Its front claws are longer than its rear claws and are used for burrowing or scooping.

Unlike the black bear, brown bears are not true hibernators and can easily be awakened during their winter snooze.

Sun bears—also known as honey bears—are the smallest bears in the world but some of the most aggressive.

You can recognize a sun bear by the yellow crescent on its chest.

Sun bears have flexible snouts and long tongues that are adapted for eating termites.

Like the black and brown bear, the sun bear lives in a den that consists of a cave, hollow log, or large hole.

The grizzly bear is a huge and aggressive species of brown bear that lives in cool mountain forests and river valleys of North America.

HOW THE GRIZZLY GOT ITS NAME

The grizzly bear gets its name from the fact that its short, dense fur becomes tipped with silver as the bear ages, giving it a "grizzled" appearance. But grizzlies can display a wide variety of color—from blackish-brown to reddish-blond!

The black bear is afraid of the grizzly and will stay away from areas where the grizzly lives.

An adult male grizzly can be up to 7 feet (2.1m) long and weigh over 1,500 pounds (680kg). Females are a little more than half the size of males.

Grizzly bears can run in short bursts up to 35 miles (56km) per hour—that's about as fast as a horse!

Grizzly bears have a large hump on their shoulders—actually a mass of muscles that gives the front legs extra strength.

Newborn grizzly cubs are about the size of a rat and weigh only about 1 pound (0.45kg).

Grizzlies have an extremely keen sense of smell and will stalk a scent they find appealing. Hikers straying into grizzly territory are advised not to take along any food items—not even protein bars!

DON'T FORGET YOUR BEAR BELLS!

Grizzlies will avoid encounters with humans unless provoked or unless they feel that their cubs are threatened. Hikers in grizzly areas are advised to take along "bear bells"–walking sticks with bells attached. A cautious hiker will ring his bear bells when approaching a blind curve where a mother grizzly might be lurking.

The razor-sharp front claws of a grizzly can be up to five inches (12.7cm) long.

Like other brown bears, the grizzly is not a true hibernator and can be awakened during its winter sleep.

The grizzly bear is an endangered species.

Bighorn sheep are closely related to goats. The male's large curving horns grow throughout its lifetime and never drop off. The female's horns are smaller.

The horns of the bighorn have ridges called annuli. Counting the ridges reveals the bighorn's age.

The female bighorn sheep is called a ewe; the male is called a ram. Their young are called lambs.

Rams can spend an entire day butting heads to win a ewe. Often, however, the ewe loses interest in the battle and wanders away!

Bighorn sheep are herbivores and ruminants—that is, they swallow their food without chewing it, and then regurgitate it in a "cud" before rechewing and swallowing it again.

There are about 200 domesticated breeds of horses in the world.

Horses have large nostrils that allow them to draw in huge quantities of air. Efficient respiration floods the horse with energy.

The hooves and teeth of a horse continue to grow throughout the horse's life.

The horse can twitch its ears in the direction of a sound to more accurately determine its source.

The large eyes of a horse give it a wide-angle view of the world—useful for seeing predators.

The life span of a horse is about 25 to 30 years.

A mare is an adult female horse. A stallion is an adult male. A foal is a horse not yet one year old. A colt refers to a young male horse, and a filly is a young female.

Always on the watch, horses sleep standing up. But fenced-in horses, feeling safe, will often sleep lying on their bellies with their legs folded under them.

Pinto means painted in Spanish, and refers to a breed of colorfully spotted horses.

American paint horses descend from horses brought from Spain to the New World, where they reverted to the wild and were eventually domesticated again.

THE PAINT HORSES:
PINTOS, TOBIANOS, AND OVEROS

The tobiano is a paint horse (pinto) whose face is solid or has a single stripe or star between the eyes. Unlike a true paint, the tobiano's legs are mostly white. The overo is a tobiano with dark legs instead of white ones.

The paint horse was prized by Native Americans and cowboys, who used it to hunt buffalo and herd livestock.

Like a purebred dog, a true paint horse has established, registered parentage and certain minimum color requirements determined by the American Paint Horse Association.

Mustangs are wild horses that are the descendants of domesticated horses that escaped or were set free as long as 400 years ago.

Mustangs travel in small, scattered bands that live and feed on grasslands. They spend 90 percent of their time grazing.

A band of mustangs will be protected from predators by a dominant stallion.

The opossum has a prehensile (grasping) tail, and an opposable thumb on each hind foot, useful for climbing.

HOW THE OPOSSUM "PLAYS POSSUM"

When an opossum is threatened, its first strategy is to snarl and bare its teeth. It also hisses and arches its back. But if the bluff doesn't work, the opossum will do what it does best—"play possum." It falls on its side and doesn't move; its tongue hangs out and its eyes glaze over. To complete the trick, its anal glands release a foul smell that simulates the odor of a rotting corpse. The opossum can keep up the act for as much as an hour!

An opossum pretends to be dead because many predators won't eat a dead animal. Others can recognize an animal as edible only if it moves.

Other animals "play possum" as well. These include pigeons, toads, and some species of snake—like the American hognose.

Raccoons have five fingers on each foot. The fingers can grasp, twist, and execute a number of fine motor functions.

The dark circles (bandit's mask) around a raccoon's eyes make the animal seem fiercer to predators.

Raccoons have neither a bandit's mask nor a striped tail until they are about a week old.

The ringed tail of the raccoon is used in a variety of mating signals. It's also used to frighten predators.

The sloth moves so slowly that green algae can grow undisturbed on its fur.

The biggest squirrel is the Indian giant squirrel, which reaches a length of 36 inches (92cm).

Baby squirrels are born in nests—usually cavities in trees. Squirrels also hibernate in nests during the winter.

There are more than 200 species of squirrel and they live in a variety of habitats. Among the most common are the tree squirrels with bushy tails; ground squirrels with slender tails; and flying squirrels, which have a flap of loose skin that connects their front and back legs.

The flying squirrel doesn't really fly, but glides from tree to tree using its flap of loose skin as an airfoil. When the squirrel hits a tree, it grips it with all four feet.

Flying squirrels use their tails to help them steer as they glide.

A flying squirrel can glide up to 150 feet (46m).

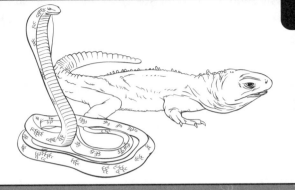

9

We should be thankful that about 200 million years of evolution separates us from our iguana-like ancestors. These days, most people prefer living in houses, not under rocks. But don't get too cozy—because of vanishing natural resources, the days of the primate are numbered. The future belongs to—guess who?—the reptiles and their cousins, the amphibians. So prepare yourself, the world of tomorrow will have a lot more of the creatures described next.

269

Like all reptiles, snakes are cold-blooded, meaning that they rely on the heat of the sun and cool of the shade to regulate their body temperature.

A snake can't remain at an extreme body temperature—either hot or cool—all day. A variation in body temperature is necessary to keep the snake healthy and alert.

An overheated snake will become listless—a sign of heat-exhaustion.

If a snake is born with two heads, the heads will fight each other for food.

The spine of a snake is made up of more than 400 vertebrae surrounded by hundreds of muscles.

Snakes have no eyelids.

You can usually tell the sex of a snake by the shape of its body. Male snakes have thick, low bodies that suddenly taper at their tails. Females have thinner, more gradually tapered bodies.

You can tell that a snake is ready to shed its skin by the clouding of its eyes. The eyes cloud, then clear, at which time the skin begins to peel away near the snake's lips. Snakes shed every one to three months.

A full-grown snake can shed its skin in only about 10 minutes.

Snakes can expand their mouths in order to swallow large prey. Their lower jawbone disconnects from the upper jawbone and drops down. After stretching its mouth over the food, the snake works its upper and lower jaws together, using its teeth to anchor and pull the food inward.

Snakes need to eat only about once a week. Some larger snakes, like pythons, eat only a couple of times a year!

Snakes have poor vision and hearing, but use their tongues to detect scents in the surrounding air.

Special bones in a snake's head amplify sound.

SNAKE LOCOMOTION

Most snakes move forward with a side-to-side motion. The snake bends into an S-shape and then stretches and contracts its muscles on alternate sides of its body. This propels the snake forward—both on land and in water. A slow-moving snake uses a different motion, that of undulating muscles along the length of its body so that it creeps forward, caterpillar-like.

The forked tongue of a snake allows it to smell in "stereo."

There are 16 types of rattlesnakes, in various colors and patterns. All have the joined rattle appendage at the tail.

In cooler areas, rattlers group together along rocky ledges to hibernate for the winter, returning to the same "dens" every year.

Unlike egg-laying snakes, female rattlesnakes keep the eggs in their bodies until they are hatched. The fully formed young snakes are born alive.

The average female rattler can contain as many as 20 eggs, only about half of which will survive.

Sometimes a female rattler is killed with the newly hatched babies still in her body. This probably gave rise to the folktale that a rattler will swallow her babies to protect them from danger.

A rattlesnake doesn't like to strike and will first warn a predator by doing what it does best—rattling!

A rattler strikes to stun rather than to hold its prey. When the fangs penetrate the flesh of a lizard or rodent, venom is injected through them.

Captive rattlesnakes don't require live food and will eat freshly killed or even frozen food, if thoroughly thawed.

Scientists have extracted a useful drug from snake venom that's used to keep blood from clotting. This drug is valuable to stroke victims.

The king cobra is the largest venomous snake. Its powerful venom can even kill an elephant!

You can recognize a cobra by the hood around its head. The cobra expands the hood—which makes its head look larger—when threatened. The hood also has false eye spots to further scare potential attackers.

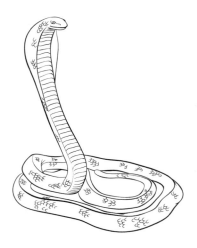

The cobra continues to grow throughout its lifetime.

Cobras can travel on land and in trees, and are excellent swimmers. If the environment is right, they can live almost anywhere. This is probably why more people are bitten by cobras than any other poisonous snakes.

Vipers differ from other snakes in that they have a thicker body, flat head, and elliptical pupils. The fangs are attached to movable bones that allow them to be retracted when the viper closes its mouth.

Saw-scale vipers get their name from their habit of rubbing up against one another. The friction of their rough scales creates a sound like a saw cutting wood.

Pythons have no poison fangs and suffocate their prey by squeezing it to death. They live in trees and feed on passing animals like small deer or pigs.

The python has special heat-sensing bumps along its lips. These allow it to detect small differences in temperature and hunt down warm-blooded prey.

Some species of python protect themselves from predators by curling into a ball and hiding their heads in the center. This arrangement not only protects the python's most vulnerable part—its head—but makes it difficult for any animal to grip the snake and carry it off.

Pythons swallow their prey whole, and head-first.

The greatest length ever recorded for a python was 32 feet (9.75m).

The South American anaconda is the largest snake of the boa constrictor family. The largest specimen ever recorded was 62 feet (18.9m) long and a foot (30.5cm) in diameter.

Anacondas live in water and have been mistaken for sea serpents or sea monsters. In fact, sightings of the famous Loch Ness monster describe an animal much like an anaconda.

Since an anaconda's weight is supported by water, it can grow much larger than land-based snakes, or snakes that make their homes in trees.

In addition to suffocating its victims by crushing, the anaconda will sometimes drown a victim by dragging it into the water.

The horned lizard of the U.S. desert has a strange way of scaring away predators—it squirts blood from its eyes. It does this by increasing the blood pressure in its sinuses until they actually burst and release the blood in a powerful jet.

A horned lizard will squirt blood only as a last resort, since it's a difficult and energy-draining activity. Most will first attempt to become invisible by making themselves so flat that their bodies have no shadows.

DIFFERENCES BETWEEN CROCODILES AND ALLIGATORS

The crocodile differs from the alligator in that it lives in saltwater and has a narrow, triangular-shaped snout, upper and lower teeth that you can see even when its mouth is closed, and fine hair follicles on its skin. The alligator lives in freshwater, has a broad snout, and displays only its upper teeth when its mouth is closed.

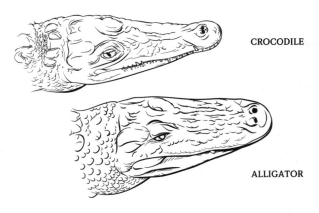

CROCODILE

ALLIGATOR

A crocodile always grows new teeth to replace the old teeth.

Crocodiles are fast learners. A crocodile caught in a researcher's trap will recognize the trap the second time around and avoid it.

Crocodiles swallow stones to help them dive deeper.

Next to the mosquito, the crocodile is the number one killer of humans in the animal kingdom.

The Australian saltwater crocodile (*Croccodylus porosus*), is the world's largest living reptile. It can reach lengths of 20 to 23 feet (6 to 7m).

A crocodile can sprint out of the water at 43 miles (70km) per hour—faster than an Olympic runner!

A crocodile's jaws don't allow it to chew, so it tears chunks of flesh from a carcass and tips its head back to swallow them.

The sex of a baby crocodile depends partly on the temperature within the nest. A warmer nest produces more males.

To regulate their body temperatures, both crocodiles and alligators yawn to let heat escape.

Alligators are among the noisiest reptiles, bellowing at each other for up to 30 minutes at a time.

An alligator can gulp down an eight-pound (3.6kg) chicken in one swallow.

The distance between an alligator's eyes, in inches, is directly proportional to the length of the alligator in feet.

Alligator skin is so thick that it functions as a suit of flexible armor. The beauty and strength of alligator skin caused the alligator population to be over-hunted. They are now a protected species.

Female alligators lay about 30 eggs inside a mound of soil and plant material that they construct by a sweeping motion of the tail. Young alligators hatch inside this mound and call out to their mother to unbury them.

A female alligator can be a very good mother. If a baby alligator is having trouble hatching, the mother will take the egg in her mouth and gently crack it open, allowing the baby to crawl out.

There are about 400 species of salamander living in freshwater and damp woodlands. They are amphibians—equally comfortable on land and in water.

Depending on the species, a salamander can have either lungs or gills. The gilled salamanders prefer water to dry land.

The Sierra Nevada salamander travels by rolling itself into a ball and bouncing along like a tire. Its soft and rubbery body softens the impact!

When not rolling, the salamander has an unusual walk—it uses its tail like a walking stick, keeping it steady on steep slopes.

REPTILES AND AMPHIBIANS—
CLOSE RELATIONS

Although also cold-blooded, amphibians differ from reptiles because they lack scales and usually return to water to breed. There are three types of amphibians: *anura* (frogs and toads), *caudat* (salamanders and newts), and *caecilian* (worm-like amphibians). However, amphibians together with reptiles make up a larger class of animals called *herps*, and zoologists who study amphibians and reptiles are called herpetologists. The word "herp" comes from the Greek word *herpeton*, which means "small creatures that crawl on their bellies."

Like other amphibians, frogs have lungs. But they also have another breathing organ—their skin! Frogs absorb oxygen directly through their skin, but they have to remain moist. They can also absorb oxygen through the lining of their mouths.

Although all frogs can jump, some can actually "parachute." Frogs that leap from great heights have extra-large webbed feet or special flaps of skin connecting their front and back legs, to slow their descent.

FROG OR TOAD—WHAT'S THE DIFFERENCE?

There are many differences between frogs and toads—some you can see and others you can't. A frog tends to be moist and slimy, with long back legs for jumping. A toad is dry, warty, and has short stubby legs for walking. While a frog lays its eggs in clusters, a toad lays eggs in long chains. Finally, toads have poison glands behind their eyes and a special plate of cartilage in their chest. Still, certain species fall into both categories—frog and toad—and it's really impossible to call them one or the other. For example, what do you call the warty-skinned frog or the slimy toad?

WHY DID THE FROG GROW EXTRA LEGS?

In the early 1990s, scientists in the United States were puzzled by the sudden appearance of frogs with extra legs. Some had as many as ten! Originally, it was thought that industrial pollution was the cause, but further investigation revealed a stranger story. *Trematodes* (tiny flatworms) live and lay their eggs in the stomachs of waterfowl, like the heron. Excreted trematode eggs fall into water where they're eaten by snails. Once inside the snails, the eggs hatch and begin to develop, eventually outgrowing their snail hosts. Sooner or later, baby trematode worms burst from the snails and look for a new host: the tender flesh of the tadpole. The worms burrow into the developing limb buds of the tadpole, causing the buds to fragment. The tadpole repairs the damaged bud by growing a new bud beside it—all of these eventually turn into multiple frog legs. The strangest part of this cycle is that multilegged frogs are clumsy and easily eaten by herons—and the whole cycle repeats!

Certain species of frogs can survive subzero temperatures, even if they're completely encased in a block of ice. The frogs produce a special protein that acts as a kind of antifreeze, keeping the water in the frog's body from freezing.

A group of frogs is called an army. A group of toads is called a knot.

A single poison-arrow frog, found in the Amazon rainforest, has enough nerve toxin to kill about 2,500 people.

Frogs will sometimes keep friendly company with—of all things—tarantulas! The tarantula shares its burrow with small frogs that keep it free of ants and other insects that might eat the spider's eggs.

The green iguanas of certain West Indian islands are called "tree chickens" by the locals. Iguanas are edible reptiles and their tails are considered a delicacy there.

The throat pouch of an iguana is called a dewlap.

An iguana can stay underwater for 30 minutes.

Lizards make up the largest group of reptiles. Most are four-legged, but a few have only two legs and others are legless. Lizards live in diverse environments and are the most geographically widespread of the reptiles.

To swim, an iguana pulls its legs close to its body, making it more hydrodynamic. It uses its tail to propel itself through the water.

Komodo dragons are the world's largest lizards. They can read reach 10 feet (3m) in length and weigh 300 pounds (135kg).

The dragons are found only on four small Indonesian islands: Komodo, Rintja, Padar, and Flores.

The Komodo dragon is a fast runner for its size. It can reach speeds of up to 11 miles (18km) per hour. It's also an excellent tree climber and swimmer.

Komodo dragons kill their prey by infecting them. The bacteria in the dragon's mouth cause a bitten animal to sicken and die within a day. The dragon then returns to the animal and eats it.

Komodo dragons were discovered and named in 1912 after numerous reports of "land crocodiles" on Komodo island led researchers to investigate.

The Gila monster was named for the Gila River basin in the southwestern United States, where the slow-moving lizard was first found.

The Gila is the only poisonous lizard found in North America.

The Gila can live for months without food. During winter hibernation, it lives off fat stored in its tail.

The Gila produces a potent venom in glands located in its lower jaw. When the Gila bites an animal, the venom flows into the animal through grooved teeth.

The venom of the Gila will rarely kill a healthy adult.

The Gila has a life span of about 20 years.

The slow worm (*Anguis fragilis*) is a legless lizard that looks like a snake. It differs from the snake in that it has a stiffer body, a breakable tail, and closable eyelids.

If caught from behind by a predator, the slow worm wriggles violently so that its tail breaks off and it can escape. A new tail regrows in a couple of weeks, but it's only about two-thirds as long as the original one.

Unlike many snakes, the slow worm's fine-scaled skin is a solid green, gray, or yellow and has few, if any, patterns. The slow worm usually grows to be about 20 inches (50cm) long.

The slow worm is common in Europe, where it can be found in fields, meadows, and pastures.

A group of turtles is called a bale.

Turtles and tortoises have no vocal chords. They can make only hissing and gurgling sounds.

**TURTLE AND TORTOISE—
WHAT'S THE DIFFERENCE?**

Although most people consider the turtle and tortoise to be the same type of creature, there's a difference. A turtle is mostly a water-dweller, while a tortoise lives on land, going to the water only to drink and bathe. Tortoises are also generally larger, having high-domed shells and elephant-shaped hind legs.

Turtles and tortoises have sharp beaks instead of teeth. Baby tortoises hatch from their eggs using an egg-tooth or caruncle, which is a modified scale, not a real tooth. But the egg-tooth disappears a few months after the tortoise hatches.

The upper part of the turtle and tortoise shell is called the carapace. The lower part is called the plastron.

Both turtles and tortoises lay eggs. The male turtle stays in the water his entire life, but the female will leave the water briefly to lay her eggs.

The correct term for turtle and tortoise hibernation is "brumation." This reflects the fact that turtles and tortoises don't undergo the same physiological changes that occur when mammals hibernate.

Since a turtle's immune system shuts down when it brumates, this is when it's most vulnerable to disease and infection. A turtle with an undetected sickness, such as parasites, can actually die "in its sleep."

One of the tortoise's favorite meals is rose petals.

The Galapagos giant tortoise (*Geochelone elephantopus*) is the largest species of tortoise. It can grow to over 8 feet (2.4m) long, weigh 500 pounds (227kg), and live over 100 years.

The Galapagos giant tortoise is one of the slowest moving tortoises, averaging only 0.16 miles (0.26km) per hour.

The Galapagos giant tortoise is endangered and will soon become extinct if unprotected.

It takes a baby Galapagos giant tortoise a full month to break through its eggshell and emerge.

The giant tortoise matures at about 25 years of age.

Slider turtles will often blow bubbles—aparently to amuse themselves. Once the bubbles float to the surface, they snap at them as if stalking prey.

The Madagascar ploughshare tortoise (*Angonoka*) gets its name from the plow-shaped protrusion of horn between its front legs. Males use it to ram each other when fighting over territory or a mate.

The ploughshare tortoise is on the verge of extinction because of wild pigs that eat its eggs.

The endangered North American desert tortoise lives 50 to 80 years.

Although active during the day, the desert tortoise spends most of its time underground to protect itself from the extreme heat and cold of the desert.

A healthy adult desert tortoise can survive an entire year without water.

When threatened, the desert tortoise withdraws its head and limbs so deeply into its shell that it's virtually impossible for any creature to extract it.

The painted turtle, or painted terrapin, is a common turtle species in North America. It gets its name from the bright greens, yellows, and even pinks of its carapace.

The painted turtle was once a popular house pet. But due to the presence of salmonella bacteria, the sale of the turtles is currently illegal in many places. Today, improved breeding techniques have reduced the risk of salmonella, and special chemicals added to the turtles' drinking water keep them healthier.

CHOOSY BEACH CAMPER

Green sea turtles, living off the coast of South America, hold the record for long-distance travel. At breeding time, they swim 1,367 miles (2,200km) to Ascension Island. This is because the turtles are picky about the kind of beaches they find suitable for laying eggs, and those on the island are the nearest ones that suit them.

An Australian turtle, the fitzroy, breathes through its anus when underwater.

The snake-necked turtle from Australia has a neck that extends half the length of its shell. In fact, its neck is so long that the turtle can't retract its head, but folds it alongside its shell when threatened.

The tuatara is a lizard-like reptile that lives off the coast of New Zealand. It has one of the longest life spans of any reptile—about 60 years in the wild—and it doesn't reach maturity until it's almost 20!

In the center of the tuatara's forehead is a primitive structure called a pineal eye. The original purpose of this eye is not known, and in living tuataras today, it can only distinguish between light and dark.

Some zoologists suspect the third eye on the tuatara's forehead aids it with depth-perception.

Unlike other reptiles, the tuatara's teeth are fused to its jawbone. This allows the relatively small creature—about 2 feet (60cm) long—to hold large prey firmly in its mouth and not lose its teeth.

Because of its eye design, a chameleon can look in opposite directions at the same time. The chameleon's brain processes the images independently and doesn't attempt to fuse them together.

The tongue of a chameleon can stick out two full body lengths, using a ballistic projection system of muscles. It's then drawn back into the body with a set of supercontracting muscles that is unique among reptiles.

THE AMAZING COLORS OF THE CHAMELEON

Chameleons are lizards that instantly change color by manipulating a layer of cells called the melanophores that stretches above another layer of cells, the chromatophores. The chromatophores contain all the various pigments of the chameleon's skin. But the melanophores act like little windows, opening or closing in complex patterns to reveal only one color or another. Zoologists once thought that chameleons changed colors strictly for camouflage. Now they're beginning to see that color change may also be a reflection of the animal's mood. Although the details aren't clear, chameleon color changes may signal that the creature feels angry, threatened, or ready to mate.

Dragons do exist! A lizard in Australia, called the bearded dragon, can change from light to dark in color, and flare out its throat (beard) when threatened. Depending on the species, it can be from 10 to 20 inches long (25 to 50cm).

Some species of the little lizard called the gecko can dash up a straight wall and even polished glass windows, sticking and unsticking its feet 15 times a second. It can hang from the ceiling by a single toe. It does this by means of its remarkable feet, which have about 500,000 tiny hairs on them. It's the attraction between the atoms of the hairs and the atoms of the surface—called "van der Waals forces" —that makes geckos stick to things.

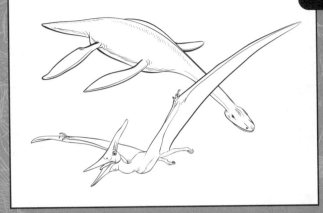

So what do the dodo bird and trilobite have in common? Both are as dead as doornails. Worse that that—both are extinct, which means that they will never again walk the face of this Earth. Nonetheless, scientists know some wonderful things about the long-vanished critters that once roamed among giant ferns and smoking volcanoes. Read on.

303

Most of the animals that ever lived on Earth are extinct.

Scientists think the first true dinosaurs lived about 230 million years ago in the Triassic Period. Dinosaurs became extinct at the end of the Cretaceous Period (about 65 million years ago). You can see that dinosaurs were around for a very long time—almost 165 million years!

The word "dinosaur" was created by the British scientist Sir Richard Owen in 1842. He combined the Greek words *deinos*, meaning "terrible," with *saurus* for "lizard."

There are currently more than 800 named species of dinosaurs with a new species discovered from fossils nearly every month. Most of these species were discovered in the last 20 years.

Dinosaurs lived on all of the continents. About 230 million years ago, the continents we now know were arranged together as a single supercontinent called Pangaea. During the 165 million years of dinosaur existence, this supercontinent slowly broke apart and its pieces spread across the globe.

The "heyday" of dinosaurs was the Mesozoic era, a period spanning about 140 million years. The Mesozoic era is divided into three periods: Triassic (245 to 208 million years ago), Jurassic (208 to 144 millions years ago), and Cretaceous (144 to 65 million years ago).

Coprolite is fossilized dinosaur dung.

"Trace fossils" are indirect fossil remains of animals such as footprints, burrows, and coprolite.

Smaller dinosaurs like *Micropachycephalosaurus* and *Echinodon* probably traveled in herds for protection. This may also have been true for the larger plant-eating dinosaurs like the *Seismosaurus*. But the large meat-eaters, like the *Tyrannosaurus rex*, traveled alone.

Plant-eating, or herbivorous, dinosaurs had stones in their stomachs. The stones, called gastroliths, helped them digest roughage.

The British collector Edward Drinker Cope, in his rush to beat Othniel Marsh as the collector of the most dinosaurs, mistakenly reconstructed one dinosaur so that its head was placed at the tip of its tail instead of on its neck. His colleagues suggested that it be named *Strepsisaurus*, meaning "twisted lizard."

Predatory, meat-eating dinosaurs like the *Tyrannosaurus rex* and *Allosaurus*, continually lost and replaced their teeth.

Trilobites are one of the most abundant fossils found today. The creatures, which had hard shells and segmented bodies, existed long before the dinosaurs—about 300 million years ago! They lived in the ancient seas and show scientists that life forms were becoming complex and well adapted to their environments.

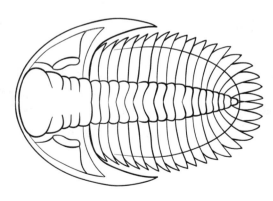

The horned dinosaur *Torosaurus* had the longest skull of any land animal. It was 9 feet (2.8m) long.

An unusual feature of the dinosaur *Tyrannosaurus rex* is a large opening on both sides of the skull called the *antorbital fenestra*. Scientists speculate that the openings made the *T. rex's* head lighter and placed less stress on its neck.

Measured from the root, the average tooth of a mature *Tyrannosaurus rex* was more than 10 inches (25cm) long.

Birds have the same basic skull design as *Tyrannosaurus rex*, including two large openings on the skull called the *antorbital fenestra*. This bolsters the theory that birds are the descendents of dinosaurs.

The raptors were a species of dinosaur with powerful hind legs and small claws. Scientists speculate that they were among the fastest moving dinosaurs and could run on two feet.

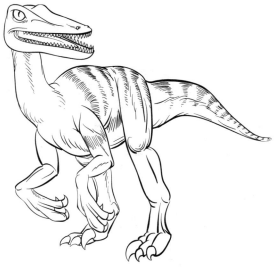

The meat-eating raptor species of dinosaurs were so vicious that scientists believe they contributed to the extinction of the slower-moving dinosaurs.

DIFFERENT WAYS TO NAME A DINOSAUR

There are different ways to name a dinosaur. Some dinosaur names combine Latin or Greek words to describe some feature or behavior of the animal, like *Triceratops*, which means "three-horned face." A dinosaur can also be named after the person who found it first, like the *Marshosaurus*, named after the 19th century paleontologist Othniel C. Marsh. Finally, some dinosaurs are named after the place where their fossils were first found or studied, such as the *Arctosaurus*, found near the Arctic Circle, and the *Yaleosaurus*, named after Yale University.

Othniel C. Marsh named at least 25 dinosaurs, including *Allosaurus* (1877), *Diplodocus* (1878), *Stegosaurus* (1877), and *Triceratops* (1889).

The name *Maiasaurus* means "good mother lizard." The dinosaur got its name because paleontologists found baby fossils next to adult fossils.

WERE THE DINOSAURS WARM-BLOODED OR COLD-BLOODED?

Scientists have long believed that dinosaurs were cold-blooded, meaning that their body temperature was identical to that of the environment. But new theories about dinosaurs suggest a different story. The paleontologist Robert Bakker believes that, to dominate mammals that created their own body heat, dinosaurs had to be fast as well as strong. He points to those fast, two-legged creatures, like the raptors, who were efficient hunters and meat-eaters. According to Bakker, only warm-bloodedness could explain the speed and power of these creatures. On the other hand, if large and slow dinosaurs like the sauropods were warm-blooded, they would've needed huge amounts of food to keep their temperatures constant. So the answer may be that the smaller, faster dinosaurs were warm-blooded, while the larger ones were cold-blooded. But since no flesh from a dinosaur has ever been found, the mystery continues.

Scientists determine the sex of dinosaurs by examining their skulls and hip bones. The males had more strongly shaped skulls and crests, which probably made them more attractive mates. The females had wider hips to allow for egg-laying.

Dinosaur life spans probably varied in length from tens of years to about a hundred years. Scientists estimate their possible maximum ages by looking at the life spans of modern reptiles, like the alligator and tortoise.

The shortest dinosaur has one of the longest names—*Micropachycephalosaurus*. It was only 20 inches (50.8cm) long. The *Echinodon* and *Saltopus* were 24 inches (61cm) long, followed by the *Microceratops* which was 30 inches (76.2cm) long.

At 150 feet (45m), the longest dinosaur was the *Seismosaurus*. It was followed by the 120-foot (36.58m) *Argentinosaurus* and the 100-foot (30.48m) *Brachiosaurus*.

The heaviest dinosaur (at least from the weight of its skeleton) was the *Argentinosaurus*. Paleontologists (the scientists who study dinosaurs) estimate that a full-grown fleshy animal weighed in at about 220,000 pounds (99,790kg).

Some fast-moving dinosaurs included the *Galliminus*, which could run about 35 miles (56km) per hour—faster than any Olympic sprinter; the *Coelophysis*, which ran at about 25 miles (40km) per hour; and the *Tyrannosaurus rex*, which probably walked at around 15 miles (24km) per hour.

According to fossil remains, one of the *Tyrannosaurus rex's* favorite foods was the *Triceratops*.

Tyrannosaurus rex was one of the most menacing dinosaurs. It had two strong, muscular legs and walked upright. Each foot had three toes with claws that could be used to tear into another animal. It was about 20 feet (6m) high and 40 feet (12m) long. A meat-eater (carnivore), it had a huge head and very sharp dagger-like teeth, some of which could be 10 inches (25cm) long.

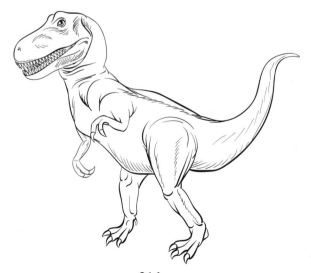

All species of dinosaur didn't all appear at the same time. The first *Apatosaurs* appeared in the middle to late Jurassic Period and died out at the end (208 to 144 million years ago). *Tyrannosaurus rex* and *Triceratops* both appeared near the end of the Cretaceous and died out when it ended (144 to 65 million years ago).

The smartest dinosaur was probably the bird-like *Troodon*, which had the largest brain in relation to its body size and lived during the last dinosaur period, the Cretaceous. Some paleontologists believe that the *Troodon* was as smart as an ostrich, which is smarter than any reptile on Earth today.

The dinosaur with the smallest brain in proportion to its body was the *Stegosaurus*. These "tank dinosaurs" were the ones with the rows of pointed plates along their backs.

DINOSAUR DIET

Meat-eating dinosaurs ate lizards, turtles, eggs, early mammals, dead animals, and other species of dinosaurs (even their own species) if food became scarce enough. But most dinosaurs were plant-eaters and munched on a variety of edible vegetation, except for grasses, which hadn't evolved yet. Rocks that contain dinosaur bones also contain fossil pollen and spores that show that thousands of different types of plants existed during the age of the dinosaur. Many of these plants had edible leaves, including evergreen conifers (pine trees, redwoods, and their relatives), ferns, mosses, horsetail rushes, cycads, gingkos, and in the latter part of the dinosaur age, flowering (fruiting) plants. Although scientists haven't figured out the exact time fruiting plants appeared, the last of the dinosaurs probably had some sort of sweet fruit available to them.

Some of the longest dinosaur names are:
  Micropachycephalosaurus (23 letters)
  Charcharodontosaurus (20 letters)
  Archaeornithomimus (18 letters)
  Eustreptospondylus (18 letters)
  Pachycephalosaurus (18 letters)

The flying reptile *pterodactyl* lived in flocks and preferred to nest in trees or caves. A place fertile with *pterodactyl* fossils is the state of Kansas in the United States.

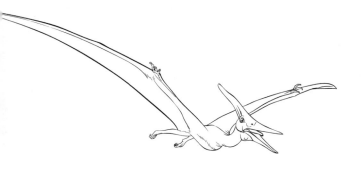

Dinosaur eggs were small relative to the size of the dinosaur's body. Even gigantic sauropods didn't have eggs much larger than the size of a basketball. This is because the bigger the egg, the thicker its shell has to be to protect it. If a shell is too thick, oxygen can't penetrate it, and the developing embryo suffocates. Also, a too-thick shell would make it impossible for the hatchling to escape the egg!

The first flying "bird-like" reptile was about the size of a chicken and had feathers. Paleontologists named it *Archaeopteryx*, meaning "ancient wing."

The *Rhamphorhynchus* was one of the largest flying reptiles—over five feet (1.5m) long and a meat-eater that preferred marine animals. It disappeared about 150 million years ago.

Recent studies suggest that some dinosaurs may have had voices. Computer studies of dinosaur skulls suggest that certain structures and chambers may have evolved to amplify and project sound. One experiment forced air through the skeletal snout of a *Tyrannosaurus rex*, resulting in a deep, honking sound.

Many paleontologists believe dinosaur skin may have had distinct patterns of coloration. This included pale bellies to reduce shadows, camouflage patterns to hide dinosaur bodies in vegetation, and bright coloration as a warning or to attract a mate.

Heavily armored dinosaurs, like the *stegosaurus*, may not have needed the protective coloration of the smaller and weaker dinosaurs.

Plesiosaurus was a flippered marine reptile that grew to about 7.6 feet (2.3m) long and may have weighed close to 200 pounds (90kg). It had four wide, paddle-shaped flippers, a tapered body, and sharp, conical teeth in long jaws. Its head was relatively small. It disappeared at the end of the Jurassic Period, 144 million years ago.

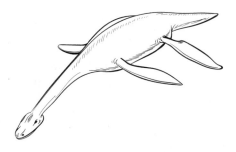

The chambered headcrests on some dinosaurs such as *Corythosaurus* and *Parasaurolophus* might have been used to amplify grunts or bellows.

TWO THEORIES OF DINOSAUR EXTINCTION

Paleontologists have two basic theories when it comes to dinosaur extinction. The Gradualistic Theory states that the dinosaurs were in slow decline due to gradual changes in their environment such as climate, vegetation, or the dominance of new predators. The Catastrophic Theory states that some huge catastrophic event, like a meteorite, led to sudden climate change that wiped out the dinosaurs fairly quickly. Whichever theory is correct, dinosaurs became extinct at the end of the Cretaceous Period, 65 million years ago.

A tiny horse called the *Eohippus* disappeared around 50 million years ago. It was only 2 feet (60cm) long and 8 to 9 inches (20 to 23cm) high at the shoulder. The *Eohippus* had four hoofed toes on its front feet and three hoofed toes on each hind foot. The first fossils of this tiny horse were found in England in 1841.

ROCKS AND AGES

Following the Mesozoic Age—the age of the dinosaurs—paleontologists have identified later ages during which important animals appeared and became extinct. These are the Eocene Age (55 to 38 million years ago), the Miocene Age (20 to 5 million years ago), the Pliocene Age (5 to 1.5 million years ago), the Pleistocene, or Ice Age (1.6 million to 10,000 years ago), and the Holocene Age (10,000 years ago to the present).

Forty thousand years ago, a crocodile called the *quinkana* lived on the land and didn't like the water. It belonged to a group of land-based crocodiles called *mekosuchines* that are now all extinct. Unlike modern day crocodiles, the *quinkana* had pointed teeth that were good for holding animals, but not good for tearing them apart. *Quinkana* would hold its prey and drown it, or shake it apart.

Megalodon was an ancient shark that may have been 40 feet (12m) or even up to 100 feet (31m) long. This is twice as long as the great white shark. The fossilized teeth of the *megalodon* are as large as an adult human hand. The shark vanished about 1.5 million years ago, during the Pliocene Age.

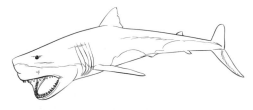

Megalodon, which means "giant tooth" had a diet that consisted mostly of whales. They ate about 2 percent of their body weight each day—a bit less than a human being eats. Sharks and other cold blooded creatures don't require as much food as warm-blooded creatures.

EXTRACTING FOSSILS

Most fossils are preserved in very hard limestone. This makes extracting the fossils on a dig site difficult. Instead, the limestone rocks are carefully cut up and moved to a laboratory. At the lab, they're soaked in a weak acid to dissolve the limestone so scientists can get a better look at the fossils.

The *ekaltadeta* was a giant rat-kangaroo from Australia, where its fossils have been found. This marsupial (pouched mammal) disappeared around 25 million years ago. It ate both meat and vegetation.

The *yalkaparidon* was a marsupial that lived about 15 million years ago in Australia. It was nicknamed the "thingodonta" because its skull and teeth are completely unlike any other marsupial known. Its fossil remains show an animal about 2 feet (61cm) long.

The *fangaroo*, which also roamed Australia about 15 million years ago, was given its name because of its huge dog-like teeth. But this small kangaroo-like creature didn't eat meat and may have used its fangs as a defense against predators.

The Bluff Downs giant python lived in Australia during the Pliocene Age, about 4 million years ago. Paleontologists estimate that it was about 33 feet (10m) long, which would have made it longer than the world's two longest snakes in existence—the anaconda of South America and the reticulated python of Asia.

The giant ground sloth, or *megatherium*, disappeared at the end of the last Ice Age, about 11,000 years ago. It was a slow, bulky, plant-eating mammal that lived in South America. When full-grown, it was the size of an elephant. The first fossil was found in Brazil in 1789.

The *macrauchenia* was one of the earliest hoofed creatures, with a small head, long neck, and possibly a trunk. It lived during the Ice Age and disappeared when the climate warmed.

The *mastodon* was an Ice Age mammal that resembled the modern day elephant. It had thick fur to keep it warm and large curved tusks that it probably used as a "snowplow"—to push snow away in order to find food. The last of the mastodons went extinct about 11,000 years ago, when the last Ice Age ended. The warmer weather probably contributed to their extinction.

The powerful *dire wolf* lived during the last Ice Age and roamed throughout the Western Hemisphere. It became extinct when the Ice Age ended, about 11,000 years ago. Over 3,600 dire wolves have been recovered from the Rancho La Brea Tar Pits in California.

The woolly rhinoceros (*Coelodonta*) was a large Ice Age mammal that lived until about 10,000 years ago. To lessen heat loss, it had thick, shaggy fur, small ears, short legs, and a massive body. Well-preserved corpses of these animals were found in frozen gravel in Siberia. Stone Age humans hunted them and drew pictures of the rhinos on cave walls 30,000 years ago.

Taller than the tallest ostrich, the *dinornis maximus* or "moa," stood over 11 feet (3.4m) tall. Slow moving and flightless, the moa wandered the plains of New Zealand until about 1800, when humans changed their habitat and wiped out their food supply.

The original name of the moa was "Te Kura" (from the Māori for "red bird") and legends exist of these giant birds living in caves guarded by lizards, permanently standing on one leg!

The *glyptodon* (meaning "carved tooth") was a giant armadillo that lived in South America during the Ice Age, until 10,000 years ago. The first fossils of this animal were found in Argentina in 1839. A fully assembled *glyptodon* skeleton is about the size of a car!

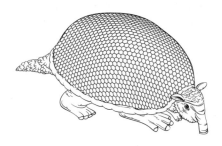

During the Pleistocene era, when South America became connected with North America, glyptodons migrated as far north as Texas and Florida in the United States. In fact, archeologists discovered a unique genus of glyptodon in Texas and named it *Glyptotherium texanum.*

EXTINCT OR ALIVE?

About 4,000 years ago, thousands of ferocious-looking Tasmanian tiger-wolves roamed the Australian outback. But despite their appearance, the tiger-wolves—which carried their young in pouches—were related more closely to kangaroos. When Asian explorers introduced the wild dingo into Australia, the smarter dingoes traveled in packs and were better hunters than the tiger-wolves. When European settlers arrived in Australia during the 18th century, they destroyed much of the tiger-wolves' natural habitat, which made food scarce. The wolves began killing the sheep of local farmers, which led to a campaign to destroy them. The Tasmanian tiger-wolves were declared an endangered species in 1936, but it was too late, and the last animal died in captivity later that year. However, five years later, based on reports that some animals still existed, the Australian government set up a 1.6 million acre sanctuary in Tasmania for any remaining tiger-wolves.

The *smilodon* was the largest of the saber-tooth tigers. Paleontologists easily recognize *smilodon* fossils because of the two huge saber-shaped teeth attached to the upper jaw. This shows that the animal was an excellent hunter. But the tiger disappeared about 11,000 years ago when the Ice Age ended. They may have died out to the warmer climate, which resulted in changes to the food chain.

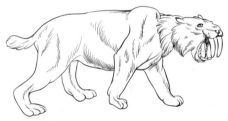

Two different types of saber-toothed tigers lived in the midwestern United States at the end of the Ice Age. The familiar saber-tooth tiger (genus *smilodon*) had enlarged canines up to 7 inches (18cm) long. The second type (genus *homotherium*) is less well-known. These cats had shorter canines—about 4 inches (10cm) long.

Japanese and Russian researchers are planning to clone a woolly mammoth from the DNA of cells they found in 2003 of the elephant-like Ice Age creature. If they are successful, cloned mammoths and their calves will live in an uninhabited region north of Russia's Kamchatka peninsula.

New estimates suggest that 10 percent of the world's 608 primate species and subspecies on three continents are in danger of extinction. An additional 10 percent might not be in immediate jeopardy but will disappear within a few decades without vigorous protection.

Insect extinction has increased in the last 20 years due to destruction of natural habitat. Scientists estimate that the vanishing rainforest has tripled the rate of insect extinction. Many of these species are helpful to the environment.

One of the most recent large animals to become extinct was the *quagga*—a hooved African desert animal related to modern horses and zebras. The *quagga* had yellowish fur with zebra-like stripes and a white mane. It went extinct in the wild in the 1870s, and the last one died in captivity in Amsterdam in 1883.

In the 19th century, there were eight subspecies of the tiger. Now there are only five. Overhunting has driven the Bali tiger, Caspian tiger, and Javan tiger into extinction.

Two animals that have become extinct since the year 2000 are the Pyrenean ibex and the red colobus monkey. The last Pyrenean ibex died on January 6, 2000 in Ordesa National Park in Spain, and the last red colobus monkey died in Africa in October of that year.

Over 200 species of fish in the Cichlid family have disappeared from Africa's Lake Victoria. They became extinct after another predatory fish was introduced into the lake in the 1960s by humans. The Nile perch was meant to be eaten, but reproduced at an alarming rate, destroying the Cichlids by both eating their young and competing for their food supply.

The sweet-tasting amanto fish once lived in Lake Titicaca in Peru—the largest freshwater lake in South America and the highest lake in the world. In 1937, as part of a federal aid package, the United States Fish and Wildlife Department introduced the North American trout into the lake for "better fishing." Within five years, the amanto completely disappeared from the lake—the only place on Earth where it had ever existed.

Thirty percent of all fishes have been listed as threatened.

The Caribbean monk seal was first described by Columbus in 1493 during his voyage to the Americas. During the 1600s, monk seals were overhunted by Spaniards who had come to the Caribbean. The monk seal was already rare by the 1700s, but the species survived into this century. The last monk seal was believed to have been killed in 1922 off the coast of Key West in Florida.

Possible sightings of the Caribbean monk seal have been reported in the West Indies since 1922. Some of these sightings have come from remote islands where it's difficult to determine their veracity. To date, organized survey expeditions have not been able to locate evidence of living monk seals, and scientists believe the date of final extinction for this species was around 1960.

The blue pike has completely vanished from the Great Lakes region of the United States and Canada. Between 1885 and 1962, over a billion pounds of blue pike were caught by commercial fishermen. Overfishing, along with increased pollution, destruction of wetlands, and the damming of tributary rivers, all contributed to the destruction of the clear water habitat the pike required to survive.

Not too long ago, the passenger pigeon was one of the most abundant bird species on earth. In the early 1800s, there were more passenger pigeons than all other North American birds combined! But by 1914, that population had been reduced to one bird, Martha, which died in a Cincinnati Zoo. The passenger pigeon was driven to extinction by uncontrolled commercial hunting for their meat. The migration and nesting behavior of the passenger pigeons made them easy to hunt in large numbers.

THE VANISHED AUKS

About a thousand years ago the great auk ranged from Canada to Norway, including the United Kingdom and Ireland. This 29½ inch (75cm) auk was the only auk species that was unable to fly, although it was as able as a penguin in the water. These birds were easy to hunt for their meat, which was a favorite of European fishermen and whalers. The feathers of the great auk were also popular and used for hats. The last great auk hunt took place on June 3, 1844, when a pair was beaten to death and their egg was broken.

America's only native parrot, the Carolina Parakeet, lived over much of the eastern United States. As settlers farmed more land, the parakeets flocked to it, eating the crops. The settlers easily killed the birds since, when one of the flock was shot, the others gathered around it instead of flying away. The last Carolina parakeet died in 1918.

THE FATE OF THE DODO

The fate of the dodo bird is probably one of the most famous extinction tales of all times. This gentle bird lived on the island of Mauritius in the Indian Ocean where, because of few predators, it had lost its ability to fly.

In 1505, the Portuguese became the first people to visit the island because it was a convenient stopover for ships traveling the spice trade. Other ships followed, and the dodo quickly became a source of food—both for its meat and for its eggs. Later, when the Dutch used the island as a penal colony, pigs and monkeys were brought to the island along with the convicts. Many of the ships that came to Mauritius also had uninvited rats aboard, many of which escaped onto the island. So along with humans, the rats, pigs, and monkeys all preyed on the vulnerable dodo. By 1681 the last dodo bird had been killed.

Index

342